D1462914

FAMILY WISDOM

Dear Partner,

The family relationship is a parallel truth to the unity and love our Savior Jesus Christ has for His Body, the Church.

The home and family was intended to be the perfect example and manifestation of joy and well-being for every living human being on the face of this earth.

Satan is launching an all-out attack against families. If Satan can successfully destroy family relationships...the home as God designed and ordained it, he has accomplished a sinister corruption that strikes at the very foundation of life as God so beautifully planned.

The truths and principles we are presenting in this book are entirely from the Word of God for your instruction and guidance.

We pray that these words will penetrate the very depths of your being...your heart, mind and soul, that you and your family will experience total victory in relationships.

As God's chosen servant and endtime prophet, I want to lift up your needs before the throne of God and for Jesus to intercede on your behalf.

We count it a privilege to pray for any need you and your family may have. Write to me today and feel free to share all your family needs with us...for you and all your loved ones.

> *"When wisdom enters your heart, and knowledge is pleasant to your soul, discretion will preserve you; understanding will keep you..."*
> *(Proverbs 2:10-11)*

God bless you...we love you more than words can say.

Morris and Theresa Cerullo

P.S. If your need is **urgent**, call our 24-hour I-CARE prayer line **(619)277-0331**.

Morris Cerullo World Evangelism • Box 700 • San Diego, CA 92138

Precious Wisdom for the Family

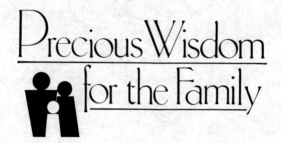

Precious Wisdom for the Family

from the New King James Version

THOMAS NELSON PUBLISHERS
Nashville

Published in Nashville, Tennessee, by Thomas Nelson, Inc., and distributed in Canada by Lawson Falle, Ltd., Cambridge, Ontario.

Printed in the United States of America.

Scripture quotations are from THE NEW KING JAMES VERSION. Copyright © 1979, 1980, 1982, Thomas Nelson, Inc., Publishers.

ISBN 0–8407–7084–7

2 3 4 5 6 7 8—92 91 90 89

Choose for yourselves this day whom you will serve. . . . But as for me and my house, we will serve the Lord.

Joshua 24:15

Contents

Contents

Introduction

But the mercy of the Lord is from
   everlasting to everlasting
On those who fear Him,
And His righteousness to children's
   children,
To such as keep His covenant,
And to those who remember His
   commandments to do them (Ps. 103:17–18).

God's promises to the family are precious
indeed. Since He instituted the family, He best
understands how it ought to function.
Therefore, the Bible is filled with inspired
advice and divine teaching about family living.
These take the form of instructions,
exhortations, commandments and warnings. In
each case the Scripture urges us to experience
God's best for our families.

This study is designed to point the reader
directly to Scripture for the answers to such
issues as dating, engagement, marriage, love,
sex, parenting, children, homemaking and
finances. Each section has a brief introduction
followed by carefully selected Scriptures. It is
intended to let the Bible speak for itself on

9

these matters. Therefore, interpretive comments are minimal. If you are genuinely seeking God's guidance on these matters, you will find it clearly stated in the passages we have selected.

The Christian family is one of our greatest national assets. It is the basic foundation of society and it is the core of fellowship in the Church. The love of God and the fellowship of the Spirit are first and foremost to be found in the family. Only when our families are what they ought to be can our churches and society itself be what they ought to be.

In a time when the family is under attack, it is more important than ever that we re-examine what the family is all about. You may be surprised to discover that the Bible speaks clearly and powerfully to every practical issue of basic family living. There is hardly a family subject that the Scripture does not address plainly and directly.

One of the keys to family happiness is *love*. It is the expression of God's presence in the home. Whether it is loving God or one another, we all need to learn how to love. Another key is learning to *forgive*. None of us are beyond the capacity of hurting one another. We all need to understand how to ask forgiveness and how to grant it. A third key is *joy*. Every family needs the joy of the Lord to bring heavenly happiness to the routine of daily living.

God provides every quality necessary for marital happiness and family harmony through the work of His Spirit in our lives. As we are controlled by the Holy Spirit, we experience His spiritual blessings in our families. He fills us with the fruit of love, joy, peace, patience, kindness, goodness, faithfulness, gentleness and self-control (Gal. 5:22–23).

As you read from the Scripture selections in this study, you will find they are arranged topically with various subheadings under each general subject. The material may be used as a biblical resource on family living or you may simply choose to read a particular section for your own devotional purposes. Each chapter is a complete study in itself and may be read individually or sequentially. May these selected passages from the New King James Version be a help and encouragement to you personally and to your entire family.

= 1 =

Marriage

Marriage is the lawful union of a man and woman as husband and wife. It is the foundational relationship of all family life. In many ways the success of a family depends on the quality of the marriage and the depth of commitment expressed by both husband and wife.

The Bible clearly states that marriage was instituted by God Himself. Recognizing man's need for companionship, God created both man and woman and blessed their union from the beginning. Despite the tragic effect of sin on the human race, marriage is often a touch of heaven on earth. In fact, it is an illustration of our relationship to Christ. He is pictured in Scripture as the Bridegroom and the Church is pictured as His Bride.

Since God is the author of marriage, He best understands how it works. Therefore, the Bible is filled with positive and practical advice about marriage and family living. The Scripture says "God is love" (1 John 4:7) and that the fruit of the Spirit is love (Gal. 5:22). He

13

is the source of love Who fills our hearts with love for one another.

Happy marriages don't just happen; they are made by love, devotion, commitment and fidelity. The marriage vow itself is a covenant between the couple and God. It is a pledge of themselves to each other to live as man and wife and raise a family to the glory of God. The vow is also a pledge to Christ Himself, Who is Lord of the family and Head of the home. With Him in control your marriage can be a reflection of His glory on earth.

Marriage Was Instituted by God

Marriage Is Blessed by God

Marriage *is* honorable among all, and the bed undefiled; but fornicators and adulterers God will judge (Heb. 13:4).

God Created Male and Female

So God created man in His *own* image; in the image of God He created him; male and female He created them. Then God blessed them, and God said to them, "Be fruitful and multiply; fill the earth and subdue it; have dominion over the fish of the sea, over the birds of the air, and over every living thing that moves on the earth" (Gen. 1:27–28).

God Recognized the Need for Companionship

And the Lord God said, "*It is* not good that man

should be alone; I will make him a helper comparable to him" (Gen. 2:18).

Two *are* better than one,
Because they have a good reward for their labor.
For if they fall, one will lift up his companion.
But woe to him *who is* alone when he falls,
For *he has* no one to help him up.

Again, if two lie down together, they will keep
   warm;
But how can one be warm *alone*?
Though one may be overpowered by another, two
   can withstand him.
And a threefold cord is not quickly broken
   (Eccles. 4:9–12).

God Established the First Marriage

And the LORD God caused a deep sleep to fall on Adam, and he slept; and He took one of his ribs, and closed up the flesh in its place. Then the rib which the LORD God had taken from man He made into a woman, and He brought her to the man. And Adam said:

> "This *is* now bone of my bones
>   And flesh of my flesh;
>   She shall be called Woman,
>   Because she was taken out of Man."

Therefore a man shall leave his father and mother and be joined to his wife, and they shall become

15

one flesh. And they were both naked, the man and his wife, and were not ashamed (Gen. 2:21–25).

God Acknowledges the Need for Marriage

And Jesus answered and said to them, "The sons of this age marry and are given in marriage" (Luke 20:34).

God Intended for Marriage to be Permanent

And He answered and said to them, "Have you not read that He who made *them* at the beginning *'made them male and female,'* and said, *'For this reason a man shall leave his father and mother and be joined to his wife, and the two shall become one flesh'*? So then, they are no longer two but one flesh. Therefore what God has joined together, let not man separate" (Matt. 19:4–6).

Marriage Is a Covenant of Companionship

Covenant of Marriage

". . . Between you and the wife of your youth . . . she is your companion and your wife by covenant" (Mal. 2:14).

Violation of the Covenant

Who forsakes the companion of her youth,
And forgets the covenant of her God (Prov. 2:17).

Or do you not know that he who is joined to a harlot is one body *with her*? For *"The two,"* He says, *"shall become one flesh"* (1 Cor. 6:16).

Unity of the Covenant

"So then, they are no longer two, but one flesh" (Matt. 19:6).

"For this reason a man shall leave his father and mother and be joined to his wife, and the two shall become one flesh" (Eph. 5:31).

Legality of the Covenant

For the woman who has a husband is bound by the law to *her* husband as long as he lives. But if the husband dies, she is released from the law of *her* husband (Rom. 7:2).

A wife is bound by law as long as her husband lives; but if her husband dies, she is at liberty to be married to whom she wishes, only in the Lord (1 Cor. 7:39).

Commitment of the Covenant

"Here is Rebekah before you; take *her* and go, and let her be your master's son's wife, as the LORD has spoken. . . ." Then they called Rebekah and said to her, "Will you go with this man?" And she said, "I will go" (Gen. 24:51,58).

Live joyfully with the wife whom you love all the days of your vain life which He has given you under the sun, all your days of vanity; for that *is* your portion of life, and in the labor which you perform under the sun (Eccles. 9:9).

When you make a vow to God, do not delay to pay
   it;
For *He has* no pleasure in fools.
Pay what you have vowed.
It is better not to vow than to vow and not pay
   (Eccles. 5:4–5).

Marriage Is Based Upon Fidelity

Fidelity Begins in Youth

We have a little sister,
And she has no breasts.
What shall we do for our sister
In the day when she is spoken for?
If she *is* a wall,
We will build upon her
A battlement of silver;
And if she *is* a door,
We will enclose her
With boards of cedar.
I *am* a wall,
And my breasts like towers;
Then I became in his eyes
As one who found peace (Song of Sol. 8:8–10).

Fidelity Is Pledged in Marriage

But Ruth said: "Entreat me not to leave you,
Or to turn back from following after you;
For wherever you go, I will go;
And wherever you lodge, I will lodge;
Your people *shall be* my people,

And your God, my God,
Where you die, I will die,
And there will I be buried.
The LORD do so to me, and more also,
If *anything but* death parts you and me"
    (Ruth 1:16–17).

Fidelity Must Be Maintained
Drink water from your own cistern,
And running water from your own well.
Should your fountains be dispersed abroad,
Streams of water in the streets?
Let them be only your own,
And not for strangers with you.
Let your fountain be blessed,
And rejoice with the wife of your youth.
As a loving deer and a graceful doe,
Let her breasts satisfy you at all times;
And always be enraptured with her love.
For why should you, my son, be enraptured by an
    immoral woman,
And be embraced in the arms of a seductress?
    (Prov. 5:15–20).

When wisdom enters your heart,
And knowledge is pleasant to your soul,
Discretion will preserve you;
Understanding will keep you,
To deliver you from the immoral woman,
From the seductress *who* flatters with her words,
Who forsakes the companion of her youth,

And forgets the covenant of her God
(Prov. 2:10–11,16–17).

Marriage Is God's Plan for the Family

Mutual Commitment

. . . submitting to one another in the fear of God
(Eph. 5:21).

Husbands: Loving Leaders

For the husband is head of the wife, as also Christ
is head of the church; and He is the Savior of the
body. . . . Husbands, love your wives, just as Christ
also loved the church and gave Himself for it. . . .
So husbands ought to love their own wives as their
own bodies; he who loves his wife loves
himself. . . . Nevertheless let each one of you in
particular so love his own wife as himself, and let
the wife *see* that she respects *her* husband
(Eph. 5:23,25,28,33).

Husbands, love your wives and do not be bitter
toward them (Col. 3:19).

Likewise *you* husbands, dwell with *them* with
understanding, giving honor to the wife, as to the
weaker vessel, and as *being* heirs together of the
grace of life, that your prayers may not be hindered
(1 Pet. 3:7).

But I want you to know that the head of every man
is Christ, the head of woman *is* man, and the head
of Christ *is* God (1 Cor. 11:3).

"And if it seems evil to you to serve the LORD, choose for yourselves this day whom you will serve, whether the gods which your fathers served that *were* on the other side of the River, or the gods of the Amorites, in whose land you dwell. But as for me and my house, we will serve the LORD" (Josh. 24:15).

Wives: Submissive Helpers

Wives, submit to your own husbands, as to the Lord. For the husband is head of the wife, as also Christ is head of the church; and He is the Savior of the body. Therefore, just as the church is subject to Christ, so *let* the wives *be* to their own husbands in everything (Eph. 5:22–24).

Wives, submit to your own husbands, as is fitting in the Lord (Col. 3:18).

. . . that they admonish the young women to love their husbands, to love their children, to be discreet, chaste, homemakers, good, obedient to their own husbands, that the word of God may not be blasphemed (Titus 2:4–5).

Likewise *you* wives, *be* submissive to your own husbands, that even if some do not obey the word, they, without a word, may be won by the conduct of their wives, when they observe your chaste conduct *accompanied* by fear. Do not let your beauty be that outward *adorning* of arranging the hair, of wearing gold, or of putting on *fine* apparel; but *let it be* the hidden person of the heart, with the incorruptible *ornament* of a gentle and quiet spirit, which is very precious in the sight of God. For in this manner, in former times, the holy women who trusted in God also adorned themselves, being submissive to their own husbands, as Sarah obeyed Abraham, calling him lord, whose daughters you are if you do good and are not afraid with any terror (1 Pet. 3:1–6).

Husbands and Wives: Interdependent

For man is not from woman, but woman from man. Nor was man created for the woman, but woman for the man. . . . Nevertheless, neither *is* man independent of woman, nor woman independent of man, in the Lord. For as the woman *was* from the man, even so the man also *is* through the woman; but all things are from God (1 Cor. 11:8–9, 11–12).

Keys to a Successful Marriage

Attitude

And *whatever* you do in word or deed, *do* all in the name of the Lord Jesus, giving thanks to God the Father through Him. . . . And whatever you do, do it heartily, as to the Lord and not to men (Col. 3:17,23).

Finally, all of *you be* of one mind, having compassion for one another; love as brothers, *be* tenderhearted, *be* courteous; not returning evil for evil or reviling for reviling, but on the contrary blessing, knowing that you were called to this, that you may inherit a blessing. For

"He who would love life
And see good days,
Let him refrain his tongue from evil,
And his lips from speaking guile;
Let him turn away from evil and do good;
Let him seek peace and pursue it"
(1 Pet. 3:8–11).

Commitment

Trust in the LORD, and do good;
Dwell in the land, and feed on His faithfulness.
Delight yourself also in the LORD,
And He shall give you the desires of your heart.
Commit your way to the LORD,
Trust also in Him,
And He shall bring *it* to pass (Ps. 37:3–5).

Trust in the LORD with all your heart,
And lean not on your own understanding;
In all your ways acknowledge Him,
And He shall direct your paths (Prov. 3:5–6).

Devotion

Better *is* a little with the fear of the LORD,
Than great treasure with trouble.
Better *is* a dinner of herbs where love is,
Than a fatted calf with hatred (Prov. 15:16–17).

Humility

Better *to be* of a humble spirit with the lowly,
Than to divide the spoil with the proud
(Prov. 16:19).

By humility *and* the fear of the LORD
Are riches and honor and life (Prov. 22:4).

Integrity

Better *is* the poor who walks in his integrity
Than one perverse *in his* ways, though he *be* rich
(Prov. 28:6).

A faithful man will abound with blessings,
But he who hastens to be rich will not go
unpunished (Prov. 28:20).

Peace

Better *is* a dry morsel with quietness,
Than a house full of feasting *with* strife (Prov. 17:1).

And let the peace of God rule in your hearts, to
which also you were called in one body; and be
thankful. Let the word of Christ dwell in you richly
in all wisdom, teaching and admonishing one
another in psalms and hymns and spiritual songs,
singing with grace in your hearts to the Lord
(Col. 3:15–16).

Love

Love suffers long *and* is kind; love does not envy;
love does not parade itself, is not puffed up; does

not behave rudely, does not seek its own, is not provoked, thinks no evil; does not rejoice in iniquity, but rejoices in the truth; bears all things, believes all things, hopes all things, endures all things.

Love never fails (1 Cor. 13:4–8).

=== 2 ===

Husbands and Wives

The Bible has a great deal to say about husbands and wives and how they ought to treat each other. In fact, the Scripture uses the symbolism of husband and wife to illustrate the relationship of Christ to the Church (see Ephesians 5:25). His union with His bride is also a picture of the ideal union of husband and wife.

Husbands are called of God to be loving leaders, providers and protectors. Wives are called to be co-operative partners. Together they are to "share the grace of life" (see 1 Peter 3:7). Living together as husband and wife is a legal bond blessed and approved by God. It is the basic foundation of family living.

The Church today is no stronger than the families that make up its membership. And those families are no stronger than the marriages they represent. Since marriage is the foundation of family life, it is vital that every married couple learn to love and understand each other successfully.

Men and women who become husband and

wife bring different gifts, interests and concerns to the marriage. As they complement one another they add diversity and variety to each other's lives. They expand one another's world of experiences and enhance each other's growth and maturity.

Husbands: Loving Leaders

He Is the Head of the Wife

To the woman He said:

"I will greatly multiply your sorrow and your conception;
In pain you shall bring forth children;
Your desire *shall be* for your husband,
And he shall rule over you" (Gen. 3:16).

But I want you to know that the head of every man is Christ, the head of woman *is* man, and the head of Christ *is* God (1 Cor. 11:3).

For the husband is head of the wife, as also Christ is head of the church; and He is the Savior of the body (Eph. 5:23).

Love Her

Husbands, love your wives and do not be bitter toward them (Col. 3:19).

Husbands, love your wives, just as Christ also loved the church and gave Himself for it, that He might sanctify and cleanse it with the washing of water by the word, that He might present it to Himself a glorious church, not having spot or wrinkle or any such thing, but that it should be holy and without blemish. So husbands ought to love their own wives as their own bodies; he who loves his wife loves himself. For no one ever hated his own flesh, but nourishes and cherishes it, just as the Lord *does* the church. For we are members of His body, of His flesh and of His bones. *"For this reason a man shall leave his father and mother and be joined to his wife, and the two shall become one flesh."* This is a great mystery, but I speak concerning Christ and the church. Nevertheless let each one of you in particular so love his own wife as himself, and let the wife *see* that she respects *her* husband (Eph. 5:25–33).

Let the husband render to his wife the affection due her, and likewise also the wife to her husband (1 Cor. 7:3).

Honor Her
Likewise *you* husbands, dwell with *them* with understanding, giving honor to the wife, as to the weaker vessel, and as *being* heirs together of the grace of life. . . . (1 Pet. 3:7).

Trust Her
The heart of her husband safely trusts her;
So he will have no lack of gain (Prov. 31:11).

Husbands and Wives

Praise Her

Her children rise up and call her blessed;
Her husband *also*, and he praises her (Prov. 31:28).

Sanctify Her

For the unbelieving husband is sanctified by the
wife, and the unbelieving wife is sanctified by the
husband; otherwise your children would be
unclean, but now they are holy (1 Cor. 7:14).

Protect Her

"The LORD grant that you may find rest, each in the
house of her husband" (Ruth 1:9a).

Provide for Her

But if anyone does not provide for his own, and
especially for those of his household, he has denied
the faith and is worse than an unbeliever
(1 Tim. 5:8).

"In the sweat of your face you shall eat bread
Till you return to the ground,
For out of it you were taken;
For dust you *are*,
And to dust you shall return" (Gen. 3:19).

Teach Her

Let your women keep silent in the churches, for
they are not permitted to speak; but *they are* to be
submissive, as the law also says. And if they want
to learn something, let them ask their own

husbands at home; for it is shameful for women to speak in church (1 Cor. 14:34–35).

Cheer Her

Live joyfully with the wife whom you love all the days of your vain life which He has given you under the sun, all your days of vanity; for that *is* your portion in life, and in the labor which you perform under the sun (Eccles. 9:9).

"When a man has taken a new wife, he shall not go out to war or be charged with any business; he shall be free at home one year, and bring happiness to his wife whom he has taken" (Deut. 24:5).

Let your fountain be blessed,
And rejoice with the wife of your youth (Prov. 5:18).

Befriend Her

His mouth *is* most sweet,
Yes, he *is* altogether lovely.
This *is* my beloved,
And this *is* my friend,
O daughters of Jerusalem! (Song of Sol. 5:16).

I *am* my beloved's,
And his desire *is* toward me (Song of Sol. 7:10).

He who finds a wife finds a good *thing*,
And obtains favor from the Lord (Prov. 18:22).

Do Not Leave Her

Now to the married I command, *yet* not I but the Lord: A wife is not to depart from *her* husband. But even if she does depart, let her remain unmarried or be reconciled to *her* husband. And a husband is not to divorce *his* wife (1 Cor. 7:10–11).

"Whoever divorces his wife and marries another commits adultery; and whoever marries her who is divorced from *her* husband commits adultery" (Luke 16:18).

Wives: Submissive Partners

She Is of Equal Essence

So God created man in His *own* image; in the image of God He created him; male and female He created them (Gen. 1:27).

And the LORD God said, "*It is* not good that man should be alone; I will make him a helper comparable to him" (Gen. 2:18).

And the LORD God caused a deep sleep to fall on Adam, and he slept; and He took one of his ribs, and closed up the flesh in its place. Then the rib which the LORD God had taken from man He made into a woman, and He brought her to the man. And Adam said:

> "This *is* now bone of my bones
> And flesh of my flesh;

> She shall be called Woman,
> Because she was taken out of Man."

Therefore a man shall leave his father and mother and be joined to his wife, and they shall become one flesh (Gen. 2:21–24).

Her Submission Is Functional

To the woman He said:

> "I will greatly multiply your sorrow and your
>   conception;
> In pain you shall bring forth children;
> Your desire *shall be* for your husband,
> And he shall rule over you" (Gen. 3:16).

Her Submission Is Voluntary

Wives, submit to your own husbands, as to the Lord. For the husband is head of the wife, as also Christ is head of the church; and He is the Savior of the body. Therefore, just as the church is subject to Christ, so *let* the wives *be* to their own husbands in everything (Eph. 5:22–24).

Wives, submit to your own husbands, as is fitting in the Lord (Col. 3:18).

Likewise *you* wives, *be* submissive to your own husbands, that even if some do not obey the word, they, without a word, may be won by the conduct of their wives, when they observe your chaste conduct *accompanied* by fear. Do not let your beauty be that outward *adorning* of arranging the hair, of

wearing gold, or of putting on *fine* apparel; but *let it
be* the hidden person of the heart, with the
incorruptible *ornament* of a gentle and quiet spirit,
which is very precious in the sight of God. For in
this manner, in former times, the holy women who
trusted in God also adorned themselves, being
submissive to their own husbands, as Sarah obeyed
Abraham, calling him lord, whose daughters you
are if you do good and are not afraid with any
terror (1 Pet. 3:1–6).

She Is the Crown of Her Husband

An excellent wife *is* the crown of her husband,
But she who causes shame *is* like rottenness in his
   bones (Prov. 12:4).

Love Him

. . . the older women likewise, that they be reverent
in behavior, not slanderers, not given to much
wine, teachers of good things—that they admonish
the young women to love their husbands, to love
their children, to be discreet, chaste, homemakers,
good, obedient to their own husbands, that the
word of God may not be blasphemed (Titus 2:3–5).

Set me as a seal upon your heart,
As a seal upon your arm;
For love *is as* strong as death,
Jealousy *as* cruel as the grave;
Its flames *are* flames of fire,
A most vehement flame.

Many waters cannot quench love,
Nor can the floods drown it.
If a man would give for love
All the wealth of his house,
It would be utterly despised (Song of Sol. 8:6–7).

Respect Him
Nevertheless let each one of you in particular so love his own wife as himself, and let the wife *see* that she respects *her* husband (Eph. 5:33).

It is better to dwell in a corner of a housetop,
Than in a house shared with a contentious woman
  (Prov. 25:24).

It is better to dwell in the wilderness,
Than with a contentious and angry woman
  (Prov. 21:19).

Better *is* a dry morsel with quietness,
Than a house full of feasting *with* strife (Prov. 17:1).

Encourage Him
Bear one another's burdens, and so fulfill the law of Christ (Gal. 6:2).

He who finds a wife finds a good *thing*,
And obtains favor from the LORD (Prov. 18:22).

A merry heart does good, *like* medicine,
But a broken spirit dries the bones (Prov. 17:22).

Help Him

And the LORD God said, "*It is* not good that man should be alone; I will make him a helper comparable to him" (Gen. 2:18).

Every wise woman builds her house,
But the foolish pulls it down with her hands
  (Prov. 14:1).

Who can find a virtuous wife?
For her worth *is* far above rubies.
The heart of her husband safely trusts her;
So he will have no lack of gain.
She does him good and not evil
All the days of her life.
She seeks wool and flax,
And willingly works with her hands.
She is like the merchant ships,
She brings her food from afar.
She also rises while it is yet night,
And provides food for her household,
And a portion for her maidservants.
She considers a field and buys it;
From her profits she plants a vineyard.
She girds herself with strength,
And strengthens her arms.
She perceives that her merchandise *is* good,
And her lamp does not go out by night.
She stretches out her hands to the distaff,
And her hand holds the spindle.
She extends her hand to the poor,

Yes, she reaches out her hands to the needy.
She is not afraid of snow for her household,
For all her household *is* clothed with scarlet.
She makes tapestry for herself;
Her clothing *is* fine linen and purple.
Her husband is known in the gates,
When he sits among the elders of the land.
She makes linen garments and sells *them*,
And supplies sashes for the merchants.
Strength and honor *are* her clothing;
She shall rejoice in time to come.
She opens her mouth with wisdom,
And on her tongue *is* the law of kindness.
She watches over the ways of her household,
And does not eat the bread of idleness.
Her children rise up and call her blessed;
Her husband *also*, and he praises her
   (Prov. 31:10–28).

Honor Him

An excellent wife *is* the crown of her husband,
But she who causes shame *is* like rottenness in his
   bones (Prov. 12:4).

For in this manner, in former times, the holy
women who trusted in God also adorned
themselves, being submissive to their own
husbands, as Sarah obeyed Abraham, calling him
lord, whose daughters you are if you do good and
are not afraid with any terror (1 Pet. 3:5–6).

Finally, all of *you be* of one mind, having compassion for one another; love as brothers, *be* tenderhearted, *be* courteous; not returning evil for evil or reviling for reviling, but on the contrary blessing, knowing that you were called to this, that you may inherit a blessing (1 Pet. 3:8–9).

Do Not Leave Him

Now to the married I command, *yet* not I but the Lord: A wife is not to depart from *her* husband (1 Cor. 7:10).

And a woman who has a husband who does not believe, if he is willing to live with her, let her not divorce him (1 Cor. 7:13).

"And if a woman divorces her husband and marries another, she commits adultery" (Mark 10:12).

Partnership: A Co-operative Venture

Be Faithful

"You shall not commit adultery" (Exod. 20:14).

Discretion will preserve you;
Understanding will keep you,
To deliver you from the way of evil,
From the man who speaks perverse things. . . .
To deliver you from the immoral woman,
From the seductress *who* flatters with her words,
Who forsakes the companion of her youth,
And forgets the covenant of her God
   (Prov. 2:11–12; 16–17).

Be Kind

A soft answer turns away wrath,
But a harsh word stirs up anger (Prov. 15:1).

He who is slow to wrath has great understanding,
But *he who is* impulsive exalts folly (Prov. 14:29).

A foolish son *is* the ruin of his father,
And the contentions of a wife *are* a continual
   dripping (Prov. 19:13).

It is better to dwell in the wilderness,
Than with a contentious and angry woman
   (Prov. 21:19).

Be Good

Do not withhold good from those to whom it is
   due,
When it is in the power of your hand to do so
   (Prov. 3:27).

Let not mercy and truth forsake you;
Bind them around your neck,
Write them on the tablet of your heart (Prov. 3:3).

Be Wise

Wisdom *is* the principal thing;
Therefore get wisdom.
And in all your getting, get understanding.
Exalt her, and she will promote you;
She will bring you honor, when you embrace her
   (Prov. 4:7–8).

Houses and riches *are* an inheritance from fathers,
But a prudent wife *is* from the LORD (Prov. 19:14).

A gracious woman retains honor,
But ruthless *men* retain riches (Prov. 11:16).

Be Diligent

The labor of the righteous *leads* to life,
The wages of the wicked to sin (Prov. 10:16).

He who tills his land will be satisfied with bread,
But he who follows frivolity *is* devoid of
  understanding (Prov. 12:11).

Be diligent to know the state of your flocks,
And attend to your herds (Prov. 27:23).

The hand of the diligent will rule,
But the slothful will be put to forced labor
(Prov. 12:24).

Do you see a man *who* excels in his work?
He will stand before kings;
He will not stand before unknown *men*
(Prov. 22:29).

Be Gentle

A wrathful man stirs up strife,
But *he who is* slow to anger allays contention
  (Prov. 15:18).

He who is slow to anger *is* better than the mighty,
And he who rules his spirit than he who takes a
  city (Prov. 16:32).

39

But the wisdom that is from above is first pure, then peaceable, gentle, willing to yield, full of mercy and good fruits, without partiality and without hypocrisy (James 3:17).

Be Forgiving

And be kind to one another, tenderhearted, forgiving one another, just as God in Christ also forgave you (Eph. 4:32).

Rejoice with those who rejoice, and weep with those who weep (Rom. 12:15).

The discretion of a man makes him slow to anger, And *it is to* his glory to overlook a transgression
　(Prov. 19:11).

Hatred stirs up strife,
But love covers all sins (Prov. 10:12).

Be Merciful

He who has pity on the poor lends to the LORD,
And He will pay back what he has given
　(Prov. 19:17).

The merciful man does good for his own soul,
But *he who is* cruel troubles his own flesh
　(Prov. 11:17).

He who follows righteousness and mercy
Finds life, righteousness and honor (Prov. 21:21).

Be Joyful

The light of the righteous rejoices,
But the lamp of the wicked will be put out
  (Prov. 13:9).

Do not sorrow, for the joy of the Lord is your
strength (Neh. 8:10).

Rejoice in the Lord always. Again I will say, rejoice!
(Phil. 4:4).

Be Satisfied

Who satisfies your mouth with good *things*,
So that your youth is renewed like the eagle's
  (Ps. 103:5).

For He satisfies the longing soul,
And fills the hungry soul with goodness (Ps. 107:9).

The fear of the LORD *leads* to life,
And *he who has it* will abide in satisfaction;
He will not be visited with evil (Prov. 19:23).

= 3 =

Parenting

Raising children has never been easy, but it has always been rewarding. Parenting is one of the greatest joys of life. It is both a privilege and a responsibility that produces incredible blessings in our lives. The old saying that "blood is thicker than water" is true. The relationship between parent and child is a unique bond that is never really separated throughout life.

Parents are God's representatives in the lives of children. Their authority is a reflection of God's authority in their lives. Therefore, parental discipline is essential in the character development of spiritually and emotionally healthy children. Parents are instructed in Scripture to teach their children by both word and example.

Leadership is crucial in every area of life. Parents are no exception. Their ability to lead their children depends upon their willingness to follow the Lord's leadership in their own lives. As they mature in their walk with God, they are better able to lead their children to maturity as well.

While parenting may seem to be an overwhelming responsibility at times, the Bible promises "righteousness unto children's children" to those who keep God's commandments and lead by example.

Conception and Childbirth

A Gift From God

And the LORD visited Sarah as He had said, and the LORD did for Sarah as He had spoken. For Sarah conceived and bore Abraham a son in his old age, at the set time of which God had spoken to him (Gen. 21:1–2).

So Boaz took Ruth and she became his wife; and when he went in to her, the LORD gave her conception, and she bore a son (Ruth 4:13).

"For this child I prayed, and the LORD has granted me my petition which I asked of Him"
   (1 Sam. 1:27).

Then the angel said to her, "Do not be afraid, Mary, for you have found favor with God. And behold, you will conceive in your womb and bring forth a Son, and shall call His name JESUS"(Luke 1:30–31).

A Painful Process

To the woman He said:

"I will greatly multiply your sorrow and your
   conception;
In pain you shall bring forth children;
Your desire *shall be* for your husband,
And he shall rule over you" (Gen. 3:16).

Fear took hold of them there,
And pain, as of a woman in travail. . . . (Ps. 48:6).

As a woman with child
Is in pain and cries out in her pangs,
When she draws near the time of her delivery,
So have we been in Your sight, O LORD (Isa. 26:17).

A Great Reward

"A woman, when she is in labor, has sorrow
because her hour has come; but as soon as she has
given birth to the child, she no longer remembers
the anguish, for joy that a human being has been
born into the world" (John 16:21).

So Boaz took Ruth and she became his wife; and
when he went in to her, the LORD gave her
conception, and she bore a son. Then the women
said to Naomi, "Blessed *be* the LORD, who has not
left you this day without a near kinsman; and may
his name be famous in Israel! And may he be to
you a restorer of life and a nourisher of your old
age; for your daughter-in-law, who loves you, who
is better to you than seven sons, has borne him"
(Ruth 4:13–15).

So it came to pass in the process of time that
Hannah conceived and bore a son, and called his

name Samuel, *saying,* "Because I have asked for him from the LORD" (1 Sam. 1:20).

Parental Respect

The Command

"Honor your father and your mother, that your days may be long upon the land which the LORD your God is giving you" (Exod. 20:12).

The Promise

Children, obey your parents in the Lord, for this is right. *"Honor your father and mother,"* which is the first commandment with promise: *"that it may be well with you and you may live long on the earth"* (Eph. 6:1–3).

The Result

"For I have known him, in order that he may command his children and his household after him, that they keep the way of the LORD, to do righteousness and justice, that the LORD may bring to Abraham what He has spoken to him" (Gen. 18:19).

"And if a house is divided against itself, that house cannot stand" (Mark 3:25).

Parental Responsibility

Financial Security

Now for the third time I am ready to come to you. And I will not be burdensome to you; for I do not

seek yours, but you. For the children ought not to
lay up for the parents, but the parents for the
children (2 Cor. 12:14).

"If there is among you a poor man of your
brethren, within any of the gates in your land
which the LORD your God is giving you, you shall
not harden your heart nor shut your hand from
your poor brother, but you shall open your hand
wide to him and willingly lend him sufficient for
his need, whatever he needs" (Deut. 15:7–8).

"And the younger of them said to *his* father, 'Father,
give me the portion of goods that falls *to me*.' So he
divided to them *his* livelihood" (Luke 15:12).

Spiritual Heritage

. . . to an inheritance incorruptible and undefiled
and that does not fade away, reserved in heaven for
you. . . . (1 Pet. 1:4).

. . . and if children, then heirs—heirs of God and
joint heirs with Christ, if indeed we suffer with
Him, that we may also be glorified together
(Rom. 8:17).

"Then the King will say to those on His right hand,
'Come, you blessed of My Father, inherit the
kingdom prepared for you from the foundation of
the world'" (Matt. 25:34).

"But seek first the kingdom of God and His
righteousness, and all these things shall be added
to you" (Matt. 6:33).

Positive Example

The LORD is merciful and gracious,
Slow to anger, and abounding in mercy.
He will not always strive *with us*,
Nor will He keep *His anger* forever.
He has not dealt with us according to our sins,
Nor punished us according to our iniquities.
For as the heavens are high above the earth,
So great is His mercy toward those who fear Him;
As far as the east is from the west,
So far has He removed our transgressions from us.
As a father pities *his* children,
So the LORD pities those who fear Him
   (Ps. 103:8–13).

But the mercy of the LORD *is* from everlasting to
   everlasting
On those who fear Him,
And His righteousness to children's children,
To such as keep His covenant,
And to those who remember His commandments to
   do them (Ps. 103:17–18).

Let no one despise your youth, but be an example
to the believers in word, in conduct, in love, in
spirit, in faith, in purity (1 Tim. 4:12).

Spiritual Truth

"And these words which I command you today
shall be in your heart; you shall teach them
diligently to your children, and shall talk of them
when you sit in your house, when you walk by the

way, when you lie down, and when you rise up.
You shall bind them as a sign on your hand, and
they shall be as frontlets between your eyes.
You shall write them on the doorposts of your
house and on your gates" (Deut. 6:6–9).

. . . and that from childhood you have known the
Holy Scriptures, which are able to make you wise
for salvation through faith which is in Christ Jesus
(2 Tim. 3:15).

. . . when I call to remembrance the genuine faith
that is in you, which dwelt first in your
grandmother Lois and your mother Eunice, and I
am persuaded is in you also (2 Tim. 1:5).

Discipline and Respect

Train up a child in the way he should go,
And when he is old he will not depart from it
  (Prov. 22:6).

Foolishness *is* bound up in the heart of a child,
But the rod of correction will drive it far from him
  (Prov. 22:15).

He who spares his rod hates his son,
But he who loves him disciplines him promptly
  (Prov. 13:24).

And you, fathers, do not provoke your children to
wrath, but bring them up in the training and
admonition of the Lord (Eph. 6:4).

Love and Forgiveness

And may the Lord make you increase and abound in love to one another and to all, just as we *do* to you . . . (1 Thess. 3:12).

Then He said: "A certain man had two sons. And the younger of them said to *his* father, 'Father, give me the portion of goods that falls *to me.'* So he divided to them *his* livelihood. And not many days after, the younger son gathered all together, journeyed to a far country, and there wasted his possessions with prodigal living. . . .

But when he came to himself, he said, 'How many of my father's hired servants have bread enough and to spare, and I perish with hunger! I will arise and go to my father, and will say to him, "Father, I have sinned against heaven and before you, and I am no longer worthy to be called your son. Make me like one of your hired servants."' And he arose and came to his father. But when he was still a great way off, his father saw him and had compassion, and ran and fell on his neck and kissed him. And the son said to him, 'Father, I have sinned against heaven and in your sight, and am no longer worthy to be called your son.' But the father said to his servants, 'Bring out the best robe and put *it* on him, and put a ring on his hand and sandals on *his* feet. And bring the fatted calf here and kill *it,* and let us eat and be merry; for this my son was dead and is alive again; he was lost and is

found.' And they began to be merry"
(Luke 15:11–13, 17–24).

"Take heed to yourselves. If your brother sins
against you, rebuke him; and if he repents, forgive
him. And if he sins against you seven times in a
day, and seven times in a day returns to you,
saying, 'I repent,' you shall forgive him"
(Luke 17:3–4).

And be kind to one another, tenderhearted,
forgiving one another, just as God in Christ also
forgave you (Eph. 4:32).

Future Blessing

Then they brought young children to Him, that He
might touch them; but the disciples rebuked those
who brought *them.*But when Jesus saw *it,* He was
greatly displeased and said to them, "Let the little
children come to Me, and do not forbid them; for of
such is the kingdom of God. Assuredly, I say to
you, whoever does not receive the kingdom of God
as a little child will by no means enter it." And He
took them up in His arms put *his* hands on them,
and blessed them (Mark 10:13–16).

Her children rise up and call her blessed;
Her husband *also,* and he praises her:. . .
(Prov. 31:28).

The proverbs of Solomon:
A wise son makes a glad father,

Parenting

But a foolish son *is* the grief of his mother
(Prov. 10:1).

The father of the righteous will greatly rejoice,
And he who begets a wise *child* will delight in him.
Let your father and your mother be glad,
And let her who bore you rejoice.
My son, give me your heart,
And let your eyes observe my ways
    (Prov. 23:24–26).

= 4 =

Children

Children are one of God's greatest gifts to mankind. From the moment of conception, they begin the exciting journey of life with all its joys and sorrows. In time, their tiny lives will grow to maturity and most of them will have children of their own one day.

Children are both a blessing and a responsibility. They can fill your life with unspeakable joy or break your heart with tragic disappointment. Someone once said that raising children was like baking a cake—you don't realize you have a disaster until it's too late!

The Bible is filled with divine wisdom of how to raise, love and discipline children to become effective and responsible adults. It teaches us that children, like all human beings, are born with a sinful and selfish human nature that must be disciplined, corrected and regenerated by the Spirit of God.

The Bible also clearly teaches parental responsibility for the task of raising, training, instructing and disciplining children. Every parent is obligated by God to set a spiritual example before his children and bring them up in the "nurture and admonition of the Lord" (Eph. 6:4).

One means of discipline Scripture prescribes is the "rod of correction." The term *rod* comes from the Hebrew word for "branch" or "switch." It is a small neutral object that gets the message across without doing any permanent harm. The Bible also indicates that the key to effective discipline is the parent, not the child. The parent must be willing to discipline himself before he can effectively discipline his children.

Children Are a Gift from God

Heritage of the Lord

Behold, children *are* a heritage from the LORD,
The fruit of the womb *is* His reward.
Like arrows in the hand of a warrior,
So *are* the children of one's youth.
Happy is the man who has his quiver full of them;
They shall not be ashamed,
But shall speak with their enemies in the gate
(Ps. 127:3–5).

Crown of Life

Children's children *are* the crown of old men,
And the glory of children *is* their father (Prov. 17:6).

Gift of Conception

So Boaz took Ruth and she became his wife; and when he went in to her, the LORD gave her conception, and she bore a son (Ruth 4:13).

And she said, "O my lord! As your soul lives, my lord, I *am* the woman who stood by you here, praying to the LORD. For this child I prayed, and the LORD has granted me my petition which I asked of Him. Therefore I also have lent him to the LORD; as long as he lives he shall be lent to the LORD." So they worshiped the LORD there (1 Sam. 1:26–28).

Jacob Blesses His Twelve Sons

All these *are* the twelve tribes of Israel, and this *is* what their father spoke to them. And he blessed them; he blessed each one according to his own blessing (Gen. 49:28).

Elizabeth Blesses Mary

Then she spoke out with a loud voice and said, "Blessed *are* you among women, and blessed *is* the fruit of your womb!" (Luke 1:42).

Jesus Blesses the Children

Then little children were brought to Him that He might put *His* hands on them and pray, but the disciples rebuked them. But Jesus said, "Let the little children come to Me, and do not forbid them; for of such is the kingdom of heaven." And He laid His hands on them and departed from there (Matt. 19:13–15).

Children Are to be a Blessing

Her children rise up and call her blessed;
Her husband *also,* and he praises her: . .
     (Prov. 31:28).

God Uses Parental Example
to Influence Children

Negative Example

For I, the LORD your God, *am* a jealous God,
visiting the iniquity of the fathers on the children to
the third and fourth *generations* of those who hate
Me, but showing mercy to thousands, to those who
love Me and keep My commandments
(Exod. 20:5–6).

" 'The LORD is longsuffering and abundant in
mercy, forgiving iniquity and transgression; but He
by no means clears *the guilty,* visiting the iniquity of
the fathers on the children to the third and fourth
generation' " (Num. 14:18).

Positive Example

The LORD *is* merciful and gracious,
Slow to anger, and abounding in mercy.
He will not always strive *with us,*
Nor will He keep *his anger* forever.
He has not dealt with us according to our sins,
Nor punished us according to our iniquities.
For as the heavens are high above the earth,
So great is His mercy toward those who fear Him;
As far as the east is from the west,

So far has He removed our transgressions from us.
As a father pities *his* children,
So the LORD pities those who fear Him
   (Ps. 103:8–13).

But the mercy of the LORD *is* from everlasting to
   everlasting
On those who fear Him,
And His righteousness to children's children,
To such as keep His covenant,
And to those who remember His commandments to
   do them (Ps. 103:17–18).

Children Are to Honor and Obey Their Parents

One of the Ten Commandments

"Honor your father and your mother, that your days
   may be long upon the land which the LORD your
   God is giving you" (Exod. 20:12).

"'Honor your father and your mother, as the LORD
   your God has commanded you, that your days
   may be long, and that it may be well with you in
   the land which the LORD your God is giving
   you'" (Deut. 5:16).

Respect Your Elders

"'Every one of you shall revere his mother and his
father, and keep My Sabbaths: I *am* the LORD your
God. . . . You shall rise before the gray headed and
honor the presence of an old man, and fear your
God: I *am* the LORD'" (Lev. 19:3,32).

Children

Listen to your father who begot you,
And do not despise your mother when she is old
(Prov. 23:22).

Jesus Reinforces the Command

But He answered and said to them, "Why do you
also transgress the commandment of God because
of your tradition? For God commanded, saying,
'Honor your father and your mother'; and, *'He who
curses father or mother, let him be put to death.'* But you
say, 'Whoever says to *his* father or mother,
"Whatever profit you might have received from me
has been dedicated *to the temple"—is released from*
honoring his father or mother.' Thus you have
made the commandment of God of no effect by
your tradition" (Matt. 15:3–6).

Paul Reinforces the Command

Children, obey your parents in the Lord, for this is
right. *"Honor your father and mother,"* which is the
first commandment with promise: *"that it may be
well with you and you may live long on the earth"*
(Eph. 6:1–3).

Children, obey your parents in all things, for this is
well pleasing to the Lord (Col. 3:20).

Obedient Children Essential for a Pastor

. . . one who rules his own house well, having *his*
children in submission with all reverence. . . .
(1 Tim. 3:4).

. . . if a man is blameless, the husband of one wife, having faithful children not accused of dissipation or insubordination (Titus 1:6).

A Child's Nature Necessitates Instruction and Discipline

Children Are Born with a Sin Nature

. . . for all have sinned and fall short of the glory of God . . . (Rom. 3:23).

The wicked are estranged from the womb;
They go astray as soon as they are born, speaking lies (Ps. 58:3).

Behold, I was brought forth in iniquity,
And in sin my mother conceived me (Ps. 51:5).

Yet man is born to trouble,
As the sparks fly upward (Job 5:7).

Children Are Immature and Unstable by Nature

Brethren, do not be children in understanding; however, in malice be babes, but in understanding be mature (1 Cor. 14:20).

. . . that we should no longer be children, tossed to and fro and carried about with every wind of doctrine, by the trickery of men, in the cunning craftiness by which they lie in wait to deceive. . . . (Eph. 4:14).

Children Have the Potential for Growth and Maturity

And the child Samuel grew in stature, and in favor both with the LORD and men (1 Sam. 2:26).

And the Child grew and became strong in spirit, filled with wisdom; and the grace of God was upon Him (Luke 2:40).

And Jesus increased in wisdom and stature, and in favor with God and men (Luke 2:52).

The Importance of Parental Instruction

Teach Children the Word of God

"And these words which I command you today shall be in your heart; you shall teach them diligently to your children, and shall talk of them when you sit in your house, when you walk by the way, when you lie down, and when you rise up. You shall bind them as a sign on your hand, and they shall be as frontlets between your eyes. You shall write them on the doorposts of your house and on your gates" (Deut. 6:6–9).

Teach Children the Way of Salvation

. . . and that from childhood you have known the Holy Scriptures, which are able to make you wise for salvation through faith which is in Christ Jesus (2 Tim. 3:15).

Teach Children by Parental Example

And you, fathers, do not provoke your children to wrath, but bring them up in the training and admonition of the Lord (Eph. 6:4).

. . . when I call to remembrance the genuine faith that is in you, which dwelt first in your grandmother Lois and your mother Eunice, and I am persuaded is in you also (2 Tim. 1:5).

The Necessity of Child Discipline

Begin Training Early

Train up a child in the way he should go,
And when he is old he will not depart from it
   (Prov. 22:6).

Train by Example

He who sows iniquity will reap sorrow,
And the rod of his anger will fail (Prov. 22:8).

Correction Is the Goal

Foolishness *is* bound up in the heart of a child,
But the rod of correction will drive it far from him.
   (Prov. 22:15).

The Rod Is the Method

Do not withhold correction from a child,
For *if* you beat him with a rod, he will not die.
You shall beat him with a rod,
And deliver his soul from hell (Prov. 23:13–14).

The rod and reproof give wisdom,
But a child left to *himself* brings shame to his
mother. . . .
Correct your son, and he will give you rest;
Yes, he will give delight to your soul
(Prov. 29:15,17).

The Results of Effective Discipline

Love

He who spares his rod hates his son,
But he who loves him disciplines him promptly
(Prov. 13:24).

My son, do not despise the chastening of the LORD,
Nor detest His correction;
For whom the LORD loves He corrects,
Just as a father the son *in whom* he delights
(Prov. 3:11–12).

Hope

He who gets wisdom loves his own soul;
He who keeps understanding will find good
(Prov. 19:8).

Happiness

"Behold, happy *is* the man whom God corrects;
Therefore do not despise the chastening of the
Almighty.
For He bruises, but He binds up;
He wounds, but His hands make whole"
(Job 5:17–18).

Peace

Now no chastening seems to be joyful for the present, but grievous; nevertheless, afterward it yields the peaceable fruit of righteousness to those who have been trained by it (Heb. 12:11).

Wisdom

The rod and reproof give wisdom,
But a child left *to himself* brings shame to his mother
(Prov. 29:15).

We Are God's Children by Faith

Promise of Christ

"But love your enemies, do good, and lend, hoping for nothing in return; and your reward will be great, and you will be sons of the Highest. For He is kind to the unthankful and evil. Therefore be merciful, just as your Father also is merciful" (Luke 6:35–36).

Burden of Christ

"O Jerusalem, Jerusalem, the one who kills the prophets and stones those who are sent to her! How often I wanted to gather your children together, as a hen *gathers* her brood under *her* wings, but you were not willing!" (Luke 13:34).

Heirs with Christ

Now I say *that* the heir, as long as he is a child, does not differ at all from a slave, though he is master of all, but is under guardians and stewards until the time appointed by the father. Even so we, when we were children, were in bondage under the elements of the world. But when the fullness of the time had come, God sent forth His Son, born of a woman, born under the law, to redeem those who were under the law, that we might receive the adoption as sons. And because you are sons, God has sent forth the Spirit of His Son into your hearts, crying out, "Abba, Father!" Therefore you are no longer a slave but a son, and if a son, then an heir of God through Christ (Gal. 4:1–7).

Children of God

I write to you, little children, because your sins are forgiven you for His name's sake. . . . And now, little children, abide in Him, that when He appears, we may have confidence and not be ashamed before Him at His coming (1 John 2:12,28).

"And I say to you, ask, and it will be given to you; seek, and you will find; knock, and it will be opened to you. For everyone who asks receives, and he who seeks finds, and to him who knocks it will be opened. If a son asks for bread from any father among you, will he give him a stone? Or if *he asks* for a fish, will he give him a serpent instead of a fish? Or if he asks for an egg, will he offer him a scorpion? If you then, being evil, know how to give good gifts to your children, how much more will *your* heavenly Father give the Holy Spirit to those who ask Him!" (Luke 11:9–13).

=== 5 ===

Dating and Engagement

Dating as we know it today was unknown in Bible times. In those days marriages were usually arranged by the parents of the perspective bride and groom. Marriage contracts were drawn up in advance by each family and betrothal vows were considered binding until marriage. In many cases the betrothal (engagement) could only be broken by a divorce.

The Bible has much to say about engagement and pre-marital relationships. From these concepts we can draw principles that apply to the modern custom of dating. These principles serve as guidelines for dating and engagement practices.

Not all biblical marriages resulted from parental arrangement. In fact, in at least the case of Ruth, she proposed to the man (see Ruth 3:9–11). Her appeal: "Take your maidservant under your wing," was a proposal of marriage. Boaz responded with an affirmative answer: "I will do for you all that you request, for all the people of my town know that you are a virtuous woman."

In the cases of Jacob and Rachel (see Genesis 29:11–18) and David and Michal (see 1 Samuel 18:20–28) the couples were in love before they asked for parental consent. In the case of Samson and the woman of Timnah (see Judges 14:1–3), he resisted his parents' objection to the marriage only to regret it later.

Dating and engagement are important activities that prepare us for marriage. Each should be taken seriously and in an attitude of seeking God's will and blessing on the relationship.

Principles of Dating

Male-Female Attraction Is Natural

So God created man in His *own* image; in the image of God He created him; male and female He created them (Gen. 1:27).

Therefore a man shall leave his father and mother and be joined to his wife, and they shall become one flesh (Gen. 2:24).

Then Jacob kissed Rachel, and lifted up his voice and wept (Gen. 29:11).

Now Michal, Saul's daughter, loved David. And they told Saul, and the thing pleased him. . . . Thus Saul saw and knew that the LORD *was* with

David, and *that* Michal, Saul's daughter, loved
him; . . . (1 Sam. 18:20,28).

Let him kiss me with the kisses of his mouth—
For your love *is* better than wine (Song of Sol. 1:2).

I charge you, O daughters of Jerusalem,
Do not stir up nor awaken love
Until it pleases (Song of Sol. 8:4).

Pre-marital Sex Is Wrong

For this is the will of God, your sanctification: that
you should abstain from sexual immorality; that
each of you should know how to possess his own
vessel in sanctification and honor, not in passion of
lust, like the Gentiles who do not know God; that
no one should take advantage of and defraud his
brother in this matter, because the Lord *is* the
avenger of all such, as we also forewarned you and
testified. For God did not call us to uncleanness,
but in holiness (1 Thess. 4:3–7).

Flee sexual immorality. Every sin that a man does is
outside the body, but he who commits sexual
immorality sins against his own body. Or do you
not know that your body is the temple of the Holy
Spirit *who* is in you, whom you have from God, and
you are not your own? For you were bought at a
price; therefore glorify God in your body and in
your spirit, which are God's (1 Cor. 6:18–20).

Therefore God also gave them up to uncleanness,
in the lusts of their hearts, to dishonor their bodies

among themselves, who exchanged the truth of God for the lie, and worshiped and served the creature rather than the Creator, who is blessed forever. Amen (Rom. 1:24–25).

Sexual Involvement Does Not Constitute a Marriage
"'Whoever lies carnally with a woman who *is* betrothed as a concubine to *another* man, and who has not at all been redeemed nor given her freedom, for this there shall be scourging; *but* they shall not be put to death, because she was not free. And he shall bring his trespass offering to the LORD, to the door of the tabernacle of meeting, a ram as a trespass offering. The priest shall make atonement for him with the ram of the trespass offering before the LORD for his sin which he has done. And the sin which he has done shall be forgiven him'" (Lev. 19:20–22).

"And if a man entices a virgin who is not betrothed, and lies with her, he shall surely pay the bride-price for her *to be* his wife. If her father utterly refuses to give her to him, he shall pay money according to the bride-price of virgins" (Exod. 22:16–17).

Jesus said to her, "Go, call your husband, and come here." The woman answered and said, "I have no husband." Jesus said to her, "You have well said, 'I have no husband,' for you have had five husbands, and the one whom you now have is not your husband; in that you spoke truly" (John 4:16–18).

Some Are Called to be Single

His disciples said to Him, "If such is the case of the man with *his* wife, it is better not to marry." But He said to them, "All cannot accept this saying, but only *those* to whom it has been given: for there are eunuchs who were born thus from *their* mother's womb, and there are eunuchs who were made eunuchs by men, and there are eunuchs who have made themselves eunuchs for the kingdom of heaven's sake. He who is able to accept *it*, let him accept *it*" (Matt. 19:10–12).

Do we have no right to take along a believing wife, as *do* also the other apostles, the brothers of the Lord and Cephas? . . . If others are partakers of *this* right over you, *are* we not even more? Nevertheless we have not used this right, but endure all things lest we hinder the gospel of Christ (1 Cor. 9:5,12).

Now concerning the things of which you wrote to me: *It is* good for a man not to touch a woman (1 Cor. 7:1).

For I wish that all men were even as I myself. But each one has his own gift from God, one in this manner and another in that (1 Cor. 7:7).

But this I say, brethren, the time *is* short, so that from now on even those who have wives should be as though they had none, . . . But I want you to be without care. He who is unmarried cares for the things *that belong* to the Lord—how he may please the Lord. But he who is married cares about the things of the world—how he may please *his* wife. There is a difference between a wife and a virgin. The unmarried woman cares about the things of the Lord, that she may be holy both in body and in spirit. But she who is married cares about the things of the world—how she may please *her* husband. And this I say for your own profit, not that I may put a leash on you, but for what is proper, and that you may serve the Lord without distraction. But if any man thinks he is behaving improperly toward his virgin, if she is past the flower of *her* youth, and thus it must be, let him do what he wishes; he does not sin; let them marry. Nevertheless he who stands steadfast in his heart, having no necessity, but has power over his own will, and has so determined in his heart that he will keep his virgin, does well. So then he who gives *her* in marriage does well, but he who does not give *her* in marriage does better (1 Cor. 7:29,32–38).

Most Are Called to be Married

"And I say to you, whoever divorces his wife, except for sexual immorality, and marries another, commits adultery; and whoever marries her who is divorced commits adultery." His disciples said to Him, "If such is the case of the man with *his* wife, it is better not to marry." But He said to them, "All cannot accept this saying, but only *those* to whom it has been given: . . . ." (Matt. 19:9–11).

Nevertheless, because of sexual immorality, let each man have his own wife, and let each woman have her own husband (1 Cor. 7:2).

For I wish that all men were even as I myself. But each one has his own gift from God, one in this manner and another in that. But I say to the unmarried and to the widows: It is good for them if they remain even as I am; but if they cannot exercise self-control, let them marry. For it is better to marry than to burn *with passion* (1 Cor. 7:7–9).

But as God has distributed to each one, as the Lord has called each one, so let him walk. And so I ordain in all the churches. . . . Brethren, let each one remain with God in that *calling* in which he was called (1 Cor. 7:17,24).

Now concerning virgins: I have no commandment from the Lord; yet I give judgment as one whom the Lord in His mercy *has made* trustworthy. I suppose therefore that this is good because of the present distress—that *it is* good for a man to remain as he is: Are you bound to a wife? Do not seek to be loosed. Are you loosed from a wife? Do not seek a wife. But even if you do marry, you have not sinned; and if a virgin marries, she has not sinned. Nevertheless such will have trouble in the flesh, but I would spare you (1 Cor. 7:25–28).

Marriage *is* honorable among all, and the bed undefiled; but fornicators and adulterers God will judge (Heb. 13:4).

Now the Spirit expressly says that in latter times some will depart from the faith, giving heed to deceiving spirits and doctrines of demons, speaking lies in hypocrisy, having their own conscience seared with a hot iron, forbidding to marry, *and commanding* to abstain from foods which God created to be received with thanksgiving by those who believe and know the truth (1 Tim. 4:1–3).

Principles of Engagement

Engagement Is Serious and Binding

"I will betroth you to Me forever;
Yes, I will betroth you to Me
In righteousness and justice,
In lovingkindness and mercy; . . . (Hos. 2:19).

"And if he has betrothed her to his son, he shall deal with her according to the custom of daughters. If he takes another *wife*, he shall not diminish her food, her clothing, and her marriage rights. And if he does not do these three for her, then she shall go out free, without *paying* money" (Exod. 21:9–11).

For I am jealous for you with godly jealousy. For I have betrothed you to one husband, that I may present *you as* a chaste virgin to Christ (2 Cor. 11:2).

Protection of the Engagement Was Important

"'And what man *is there* who is betrothed to a woman and has not *yet* married her? Let him go and return to his house, lest he die in the battle and another man marry her'" (Deut. 20:7).

Violation of the Engagement Was a Punishable Offense

"If a man is found lying with a woman married to a husband, then both of them shall die, *both* the man that lay with the woman, and the woman; so you shall put away the evil *person* from Israel. If a young woman *who* is a virgin is betrothed to a husband, and a man finds her in the city and lies with her, then you shall bring them both out to the gate of that city, and you shall stone them to death with stones, the young woman because she did not cry out in the city, and the man because he humbled his neighbor's wife; so you shall put away the evil *person* from among you. But if a man finds a betrothed young woman in the countryside, and the man forces her and lies with her, then only the man who lay with her shall die. But you shall do nothing to the young woman; *there is* in the young woman no sin *worthy* of death, for just as when a man rises against his neighbor and kills him, even so *is* this matter; for he found her in the countryside, *and* the betrothed young woman cried out, but *there was* no one to save her" (Deut. 22:25–27).

Now the birth of Jesus Christ was as follows: After His mother Mary was betrothed to Joseph, before they came together, she was found with child of the Holy Spirit. Then Joseph her husband, being a just *man*, and not wanting to make her a public example, was minded to put her away secretly. But while he thought about these things, behold, an angel of the Lord appeared to him in a dream, saying, "Joseph, son of David, do not be afraid to take to you Mary your wife, for that which is conceived in her is of the Holy Spirit" (Matt. 1:18–20).

"And if a man entices a virgin who is not betrothed, and lies with her, he shall surely pay the bride-price for her *to be* his wife. If her father utterly refuses to give her to him, he shall pay money according to the bride-price of virgins" (Exod. 22:16–17).

Parental Blessing Was Vital to the Engagement
So he said, "I *am* Abraham's servant. The LORD has blessed my master greatly, and he has become great; and He has given him flocks and herds, silver and gold, male and female servants, and camels and donkeys. And Sarah my master's wife bore a son to my master when she was old; and to him he has given all that he has. Now my master made me swear, saying, 'You shall not take a wife for my son from the daughters of the Canaanites, in whose land I dwell; but you shall go to my father's house and to my kindred, and take a wife for my son'" (Gen. 24:34–38).

Then Isaac called Jacob and blessed him, and charged him, and said to him: "You shall not take a wife from the daughters of Canaan. Arise, go to Padan Aram, to the house of Bethuel your mother's

father; and take yourself a wife from there of the
daughters of Laban your mother's brother.
"May God Almighty bless you,
And make you fruitful and multiply you,
That you may be an assembly of peoples; . . ."
(Gen. 28:1–3).

Now Jacob loved Rachel; and he said, "I will serve
you seven years for Rachel your younger daughter."
And Laban said, "*It is* better that I give her to you
than that I should give her to another man. Stay
with me." So Jacob served seven years for Rachel,
and they seemed *but* a few days to him because of
the love he had for her (Gen. 29:18–20).

Then Moses was content to live with the man, and
he gave Zipporah his daughter to Moses
(Exod. 2:21).

Now Samson went down to Timnah, and saw a
woman in Timnah of the daughters of the
Philistines. So he went up and told his father and
mother, saying, "I have seen a woman in Timnah of
the daughters of the Philistines; now therefore, get
her for me as a wife" (Judg. 14:1–2).

Civil Authority Was Essential for Marriage
And Pharaoh called Joseph's name Zaphnath-
Paaneah. And he gave him as a wife Asenath, the
daughter of Poti-Pherah priest of On. So Joseph
went out over *all* the land of Egypt (Gen. 41:45).

So Esther was taken to King Ahasuerus, into his
royal palace, in the tenth month, which *is* the

month of Tebeth, in the seventh year of his reign (Esther 2:16).

Personal Approval Was Essential for Marriage

So they said, "We will call the young woman and ask her personally." Then they called Rebekah and said to her, "Will you go with this man?" And she said, "I will go" (Gen. 24:57–58).

Engagement Is a Time of Joy

Go forth, O daughters of Zion,
And see King Solomon with the crown
With which his mother crowned him
On the day of his espousals,
The day of the gladness of his heart
    (Song of Sol. 3:11).

Engagement Is an Expression of Love

Go and cry in the hearing of Jerusalem, saying,
'Thus says the LORD:
    "I remember you,
    The kindness of your youth,
    The love of your betrothal,
    When you went after Me in the wilderness,
    In a land *that was* not sown"'" (Jer. 2:2).

Engagement Is a Picture of our Relationship to Christ

For I am jealous for you with godly jealousy. For I have betrothed you to one husband, that I may present *you as* a chaste virgin to Christ (2 Cor. 11:2).

75

Believers Are to Marry Other Believers

"Nor shall you make marriages with them. You shall not give your daughter to their son, nor take their daughter for your son. For they will turn your sons away from following Me, to serve other gods; so the anger of the LORD will be aroused against you and destroy you suddenly" (Deut. 7:3–4).

"Or else, if indeed you do go back, and cling to the remnant of these nations—these that remain among you—and make marriages with them, and go in to them and they to you, know for certain that the LORD your God will no longer drive out these nations from before you. But they shall be snares and traps to you, and scourges on your sides and thorns in your eyes, until you perish from this good land which the LORD your God has given you" (Josh. 23:12–13).

Do not be unequally yoked together with unbelievers. For what fellowship has righteousness with lawlessness? And what communion has light with darkness? And what accord has Christ with Belial? Or what part has a believer with an unbeliever? And what agreement has the temple of God with idols? For you are the temple of the living God. As God has said:

*"I will dwell in them
And walk among them.
I will be their God,
And they shall be My people."*

Therefore

*"Come out from among them
And be separate, says the Lord.
Do not touch what is unclean,
And I will receive you."
"I will be a Father to you,
And you shall be My sons and daughters,
Says the Lord Almighty"* (2 Cor. 6:14–18).

$$=== 6 ===$$

Weddings

Weddings are always joyous and festive occasions. In a Christian context they are ideally the time when two believers are united together in Christ in the bond of matrimony. The wedding itself is the ceremony that commemorates God's leading in the lives of both bride and groom. It is also the means of legally and spiritually sanctioning the marriage.

In the Bible, references to weddings generally reflect the culture of biblical times. The oriental weddings of the Near East generally began with an initial ceremony and were followed by seven days of festivities, consumating in a great marriage supper. After a final ceremony at the end of the seventh day, the groom took the bride home and the marriage was binding.

Great emphasis is placed upon the joy and propriety of weddings mentioned in the Bible. One had to be officially invited to the wedding and had to attend in proper attire. Jesus even emphasized the importance of attending with the right attitude.

Each individual played a key role at the wedding. The center of attention was on the bride and groom. The attendants were to be prepared and waiting to serve. The best man, called the "friend of the bridegroom," not only stood at his side, but, in those days, had to be prepared to marry the bride if the groom failed to show. In all the wedding party was a picture of great joy and excitement. In Scripture this motif is used to illustrate the union of Christ and His Bride, the Church, at the marriage supper of the Lamb.

Bride: Adorned

I will greatly rejoice in the LORD,
My soul shall be joyful in my God;
For He has clothed me with the garments of
    salvation,
He has covered me with the robe of righteousness,
As a bridegroom decks *himself* with ornaments,
And as a bride adorns *herself* with her jewels. (Isa.
    61:10).

Then I, John, saw the holy city, New Jerusalem, coming down out of heaven from God, prepared as a bride adorned for her husband (Rev. 21:2).

Groom: Rejoicing

"He who has the bride is the bridegroom; but the friend of the bridegroom, who stands and hears him, rejoices greatly because of the bridegroom's

voice. Therefore this joy of mine is fulfilled"
(John 3:29).

For *as* a young man marries a virgin,
So shall your sons marry you;
And *as* the bridegroom rejoices over the bride,
So shall your God rejoice over you (Isa. 62:5).

And He said to them, "Can you make the friends
of the bridegroom fast while the bridegroom is with
them?" (Luke 5:34).

Which *is* like a bridegroom coming out of his
  chamber,
And rejoices like a strong man to run its race
  (Ps. 19:5).

Parents: Giving in Marriage

So then he who gives *her* in marriage does
well. . . .(1 Cor. 7:38).

"For as in the days before the flood, they were
eating and drinking, marrying and giving in
marriage, until the day that Noah entered the
ark . . ." (Matt. 24:38).

Best Man: Friend of the Bridegroom

"He who has the bride is the bridegroom; but the
friend of the bridegroom, who stands and hears
him, rejoices greatly because of the bridegroom's
voice. Therefore this joy of mine is fulfilled"
(John 3:29).

Attendants: Prepared and Waiting

"Then the kingdom of heaven shall be likened to ten virgins who took their lamps and went out to meet the bridegroom. Now five of them were wise, and five *were* foolish. Those who *were* foolish took their lamps and took no oil with them, but the wise took oil in their vessels with their lamps. But while the bridegroom was delayed, they all slumbered and slept. And at midnight a cry was *heard:* 'Behold, the bridegroom is coming; go out to meet him!' Then all those virgins arose and trimmed their lamps. And the foolish said to the wise, 'Give us *some* of your oil, for our lamps are going out.' But the wise answered, saying, '*No,* lest there should not be enough for us and you; but go rather to those who sell, and buy for yourselves.' And while they went to buy, the bridegroom came, and those who were ready went in with him to the wedding; and the door was shut. Afterward the other virgins came also, saying, 'Lord, Lord, open to us!' But he answered and said, 'Assuredly, I say to you, I do not know you.' Watch therefore, for you know neither the day nor the hour in which the Son of Man is coming" (Matt. 25:1–13).

"For where your treasure is, there your heart will be also. Let your waist be girded and *your* lamps burning; and you yourselves be like men who wait for their master, when he will return from the wedding, that when he comes and knocks they may open to him immediately. Blessed *are* those servants whom the master, when he comes, will find watching. Assuredly, I say to you that he will gird himself and have them sit down *to eat*, and will come and serve them. And if he should come in the second watch, or come in the third watch, and find *them* so, blessed are those servants. But know this, that if the master of the house had known what hour the thief would come, he would have watched and not allowed his house to be broken into. Therefore you also be ready, for the Son of Man is coming at an hour you do not expect" (Luke 12:34–40).

Guests: In Proper Respect

And Jesus answered and spoke to them again by parables and said: "The kingdom of heaven is like a certain king who arranged a marriage for his son, and sent out his servants to call those who were invited to the wedding; and they were not willing to come. Again, he sent out other servants, saying, 'Tell those who are invited, "See, I have prepared my dinner; my oxen and fatted cattle *are* killed, and all things *are* ready. Come to the wedding."' But they made light of it and went their ways, one to his own farm, another to his business. And the rest seized his servants, treated *them* spitefully, and killed *them*. But when the king heard *about it*, he was furious. And he sent out his armies, destroyed those murderers, and burned up their city. Then he said to his servants, 'The wedding is ready, but those who were invited were not worthy. Therefore go into the highways, and as many as you find, invite to the wedding.' So those servants went out into the highways and gathered together all whom they found, both bad and good. And the wedding *hall* was filled with guests" (Matt. 22:1–10).

Guests: In Proper Attire

"But when the king came in to see the guests, he saw a man there who did not have on a wedding garment. So he said to him, 'Friend, how did you come in here without a wedding garment?' And he was speechless. Then the king said to the servants, 'Bind him hand and foot, take him away, and cast *him* into outer darkness; there will be weeping and gnashing of teeth.' For many are called, but few *are* chosen" (Matt. 22:11–14).

Guests: In Proper Attitude

"And some fell among thorns, and the thorns sprang up with it and choked it. But others fell on good ground, sprang up, and yielded a crop a hundredfold." When He had said these things He cried, "He who has ears to hear, let him hear!" Then His disciples asked Him, saying, "What does this parable mean?" And He said, "To you it has been given to know the mysteries of the kingdom of God, but to the rest *it is given* in parables, that

'Seeing they may not see,
And hearing they may not understand.'

Now the parable is this: The seed is the word of God" (Luke 8:7–11).

Marriage Supper: Bountiful Blessing

Celebration and Culmination

He brought me to the banqueting house,
And his banner over me *was* love.
Sustain me with cakes of raisins,
Refresh me with apples,
For I *am* lovesick.
His left hand *is* under my head,
And his right hand embraces me.
I charge you, O daughters of Jerusalem,
By the gazelles or by the does of the field,
Do not stir up nor awaken love
Until it pleases (Song of Sol. 2:4–7).

Jesus Blesses the Wedding at Cana

On the third day there was a wedding in Cana of Galilee, and the mother of Jesus was there. Now both Jesus and His disciples were invited to the wedding. And when they ran out of wine, the mother of Jesus said to Him, "They have no wine." Jesus said to her, "Woman, what does your concern have to do with Me? My hour has not yet come." His mother said to the servants, "Whatever He says to you, do *it.*" Now there were set there six waterpots of stone, according to the manner of purification of the Jews, containing twenty or thirty gallons apiece. Jesus said to them, "Fill the water pots with water." And they filled them up to the brim. And He said to them, "Draw *some* out now, and take *it* to the master of the feast." And they took *it*. When the master of the feast had tasted the water that was made wine, and did not know where it came from (but the servants who had drawn the water knew), the master of the feast called the bridegroom. And he said to him, "Every man at the beginning sets out the good wine, and when the *guests* have well drunk, then that *which is* inferior; *but* you have kept the good wine until now." This beginning of signs Jesus did in Cana of Galilee, and manifested His glory; and His disciples believed in Him (John 2:1–11).

Marriage Supper of the Lamb
Then a voice came from the throne, saying, "Praise our God, all you His servants and those who fear Him, both small and great!" And I heard, as it were, the voice of a great multitude, as the sound of many waters and as the sound of mighty thunderings, saying, "Alleluia! For the Lord God Omnipotent reigns! Let us be glad and rejoice and give Him glory, for the marriage of the Lamb has come, and His wife has made herself ready." And to her it was granted to be arrayed in fine linen, clean and bright, for the fine linen is the righteous acts of the saints. Then he said to me, "Write: 'Blessed *are* those who are called to the marriage supper of the Lamb!'" And he said to me, "These are the true sayings of God" (Rev. 19:5–9).

$$=== 7 ===$$

Divorce

Once considered a disgraceful option, divorce is now tolerable, acceptable and even fashionable. For some, it is an easy way out of the responsibilities of marriage. For others, it triggers a lifelong heartbreak from which they may never recover.

The Bible clearly states that God hates divorce, yet He allows it because of the hardness of people's hearts. Jesus stated that God's original intention was to institute marriage as a permanent relationship between husband and wife. Our Lord was so committed to the ideal of permanence in marriage that He allowed only one option for divorce. The apostle Paul added another as the Church confronted this problem.

There is a great deal of debate in Christian circles over the issues of divorce and remarriage. Some believe divorce is never permitted under any circumstances. Others believe divorce is allowed, but not remarriage. Still others accept certain grounds for both divorce and remarriage. It is our intention to let the Scripture speak for itself on this issue.

In the Old Testament Moses allowed divorce and remarriage and Ezra even commanded it. Unfortunately, their permission was eventually taken as promotion of divorce for *any* reason. It was this latter idea that Jesus combatted in all of His statements about divorce and remarriage.

Divorce is not God's ideal. He invented marriage, not divorce. From the beginning, Jesus said, God intended marriage to be a permanent relationship between one man and one woman. God only allowed divorce in order to regulate it and protect the rights of the wife who was being sent away with a bill of divorcement. God's ideal is still one man for one woman for one lifetime.

God Established Marriage as a Permanent Relationship

God Created Male and Female

So God created man in His *own* image; in the image of God He created him; male and female He created them. Then God blessed them, and God said to them, "Be fruitful and multiply; fill the earth and subdue it; have dominion over the fish of the sea, over the birds of the air, and over every living thing that moves on the earth" (Gen. 1:27–28).

God Instituted Marriage

And the Lord God caused a deep sleep to fall on Adam, and he slept; and He took one of his ribs, and closed up the flesh in its place. Then the rib which the Lord God had taken from man He made into a woman, and He brought her to the man. And Adam said:

> "This *is* now bone of my bones
> And flesh of my flesh;
> She shall be called Woman,
> Because she was taken out of Man."

Then God said, "Let the earth bring forth the living creature according to its kind: cattle and creeping thing and beast of the earth, *each* according to its kind"; and it was so. And they were both naked, the man and his wife, and were not ashamed (Gen. 2:21–25).

God Intended for Marriage to Last

And He answered and said to them, "Have you not read that He who made *them* at the beginning, *'made them male and female,'* and said, *'For this reason a man shall leave his father and mother and be joined to his wife, and the two shall become one flesh'*? So then, they are no longer two but one flesh. Therefore what God has joined together, let not man separate" (Matt. 19:4–6).

Yet you say, "For what reason?"
Because the LORD has been witness
Between you and the wife of your youth,
With whom you have dealt treacherously;
Yet she is your companion
And your wife by covenant.
But did He not make *them* one,
Having a remnant of the Spirit?
And why one?
He seeks godly offspring.
Therefore take heed to your spirit,
And let none deal treacherously with the wife of his
  youth.
"For the LORD God of Israel says
That He hates divorce,
For it covers one's garment with violence,"
Says the LORD of hosts.
"Therefore take heed to your spirit,
That you do not deal treacherously" (Mal. 2:14–16).

Marriage Is Legally Binding

For the woman who has a husband is bound by the
law to *her* husband as long as he lives. But if the
husband dies, she is released from the law of *her*
husband. So then if, while *her* husband lives, she
marries another man, she will be called an
adulteress; but if her husband dies, she is free from
that law, so that she is no adulteress, though she
has married another man (Rom. 7:2–3).

A wife is bound by law as long as her husband lives; but if her husband dies, she is at liberty to be married to whom she wishes, only in the Lord (1 Cor. 7:39).

God Permitted Divorce Because of the Hardness of People's Hearts

Moses' Command

"When a man takes a wife and marries her, and it happens that she finds no favor in his eyes because he has found some uncleanness in her, and he writes her a certificate of divorce, puts *it* in her hand, and sends her out of his house, when she has departed from his house, and goes and becomes another man's *wife, if* the latter husband detests her and writes her a certificate of divorce, puts *it* in her hand, and sends her out of his house, or if the latter husband dies who took her *to be* his wife, *then* her former husband who divorced her must not take her back to be his wife after she has been defiled; for that *is* an abomination before the LORD, and you shall not bring sin on the land which the LORD your God is giving you *as* an inheritance" (Deut. 24:1–4).

Jesus' Interpretation

They said to Him, "Why then did Moses command to give a certificate of divorce, and to put her away?" He said to them, "Moses, because of the hardness of your hearts, permitted you to divorce your wives, but from the beginning it was not so.

And I say to you, whoever divorces his wife, except for sexual immorality, and marries another, commits adultery; and whoever marries her who is divorced commits adultery" (Matt. 19:7–9).

God Allowed Divorce as a Remedy for Sinful Actions

Women Taken as a Prisoner of War

"When you go out to war against your enemies, and the LORD your God delivers them into your hand, and you take them captive, and you see among the captives a beautiful woman, and desire her and would take her for your wife, then you shall bring her home to your house, and she shall shave her head and trim her nails. She shall put off the clothes of her captivity, remain in your house, and mourn her father and her mother a full month; after that you may go in to her and be her husband, and she shall be your wife. And it shall be, if you have no delight in her, then you shall set her free, but you certainly shall not sell her for money; you shall not treat her brutally, because you have humbled her" (Deut. 21:10–14).

Israelite Spiritual Inter-marriage with Pagans

And Shechaniah the son of Jehiel, *one* of the sons of Elam, spoke up and said to Ezra, "We have trespassed against our God, and have taken pagan wives from the peoples of the land; yet now there is hope in Israel in spite of this. Now therefore, let us make a covenant with our God to put away all these wives and those who have been born to them, according to the counsel of my master and of those who tremble at the commandment of our God; and let it be done according to the law" (Ezra 10:2–3).

Then Ezra the priest stood up and said to them, "You have transgressed and have taken pagan wives, adding to the guilt of Israel. Now therefore, make confession to the LORD God of your fathers, and do His will; separate yourselves from the peoples of the land, and from the pagan wives" (Ezra 10:10–11).

The Bible Gives Two Legitimate Grounds for Divorce

Unfaithfulness: Sexual Immorality

"Furthermore it has been said, *'Whoever divorces his wife, let him give her a certificate of divorce.'* But I say to you that whoever divorces his wife for any reason except sexual immorality causes her to commit adultery; and whoever marries a woman who is divorced commits adultery" (Matt. 5:31–32).

The Pharisees also came to Him, testing Him, and saying to Him, "Is it lawful for a man to divorce his wife for *just* any reason?" . . . "And I say to you, whoever divorces his wife, except for sexual immorality, and marries another, commits adultery; and whoever marries her who is divorced commits adultery" (Matt. 19:3,9).

Desertion: Religious Differences

But to the rest I, not the Lord, say: If any brother has a wife who does not believe, and she is willing to live with him, let him not divorce her. And a woman who has a husband who does not believe, if he is willing to live with her, let her not divorce him. For the unbelieving husband is sanctified by the wife, and the unbelieving wife is sanctified by the husband; otherwise your children would be unclean, but now they are holy. But if the unbeliever departs, let him depart; a brother or a sister is not under bondage in such *cases*. But God has called us to peace. For how do you know, O wife, whether you will save *your* husband? Or how do you know, O husband, whether you will save *your* wife? (1 Cor. 7:12–16).

In All Cases of Marital Separation the Bible Encourages Reconciliation

Casual Separation

Now to the married I command, *yet* not I but the Lord: A wife is not to depart from *her* husband. But even if she does depart, let her remain unmarried or be reconciled to *her* husband. And a husband is not to divorce *his* wife (1 Cor. 7:10–11).

Serious Separation

Then the LORD said to me, "Go again, love a woman *who is* loved by a lover and is committing adultery, just like the love of the LORD for the children of Israel, who look to other gods and love

93

the raisin cakes *of the pagans.*" So I bought her for myself for fifteen *shekels* of silver, and one and one-half homers of barley. And I said to her, "You shall stay with me many days; you shall not play the harlot, nor shall you have a man; thus I *will* also *be* toward you" (Hos. 3:1–3).

Remarriage Is Allowed after a Legitimate Divorce

Moses Allowed It

"When a man takes a wife and marries her, and it happens that she finds no favor in his eyes because he has found some uncleanness in her, and he writes her a certificate of divorce, puts *it* in her hand, and sends her out of his house, when she has departed from his house, and goes and becomes another man's *wife*, . . ." (Deut. 24:1–2).

Jesus Allowed It

"And I say to you, whoever divorces his wife, except for sexual immorality, and marries another, commits adultery; and whoever marries her who is divorced commits adultery" (Matt. 19:9).

Paul Allowed It

Are you bound to a wife? Do not seek to be loosed. Are you loosed from a wife? Do not seek a wife. But even if you do marry, you have not sinned; and if a virgin marries, she has not sinned. Nevertheless such will have trouble in the flesh, but I would spare you (1 Cor. 7:27–28).

Remarriage Is Prohibited in Some Cases

One Cannot Forsake a Present Marriage and Remarry a Former Partner

". . . *if* the latter husband detests her and writes her a certificate of divorce, puts *it* in her hand, and sends her out of his house, or if the latter husband dies who took her *to be* his wife, *then* her former husband who divorced her must not take her back to be his wife after she has been defiled; for that *is* an abomination before the LORD, and you shall not bring sin on the land which the LORD your God is giving you *as* an inheritance" (Deut. 2:3–4).

"They say, 'If a man divorces his wife,
And she goes from him
And becomes another man's,
May he return to her again?'
Would not that land be greatly polluted?
But you have played the harlot with many lovers;
Yet return to Me," says the LORD (Jer. 3:1).

Priests Were Not to Marry Harlots, Widows or Divorcees

"'They shall not take a wife *who is* a harlot or a defiled woman, nor shall they take a woman divorced from her husband; for the priest is holy to his God. . . .' 'A widow or a divorced woman or a defiled woman *or* a harlot—these he shall not marry; but he shall take a virgin of his own people as wife'" (Lev. 21:7,14).

"They shall not take as a wife a widow or a divorced woman, but take virgins of the descendants of the house of Israel, or widows of priests" (Ezek. 44:22).

Pastors Are to Be the Husband of One Wife

A bishop then must be blameless, the husband of one wife, temperate, sober-minded, of good behavior, hospitable, able to teach; not given to wine, not violent, not greedy for money, but gentle, not quarrelsome, not covetous; one who rules his own house well, having *his* children in submission with all reverence (for if a man does not know how to rule his own house, how will he take care of the church of God?); . . . (1 Tim. 3:2–5).

Can the Sin of Divorce Be Forgiven?

The Unpardonable Sin Is Not Divorce

"Therefore I say to you, every sin and blasphemy will be forgiven men, but the blasphemy *against* the Spirit will not be forgiven men. Anyone who speaks a word against the Son of Man, it will be forgiven him; but whoever speaks against the Holy Spirit, it will not be forgiven him, either in this age or in the *age* to come" (Matt. 12:31–32).

God Forgives All Our Sins

He has not dealt with us according to our sins,
Nor punished us according to our iniquities.
For as the heavens are high above the earth,
So great is His mercy toward those who fear Him;

As far as the east is from the west,
So far has He removed our transgressions from us
(Ps. 103:10–12).

. . . buried with Him in baptism, in which you also
were raised with *Him* through faith in the working
of God, who raised Him from the dead. And you,
being dead in your trespasses and the
uncircumcision of your flesh, He has made alive
together with Him, having forgiven you all
trespasses, . . . (Col. 2:12–13).

In Him we have redemption through His blood, the
forgiveness of sins, according to the riches of His
grace . . . (Eph. 1:7).

How Should We Deal with Those Who Are Having Marital Problems?

Approach: Honest Confrontation

"Moreover if your brother sins against you, go and
tell him his fault between you and him alone. If he
hears you, you have gained your brother. But if he
will not hear *you*, take with you one or two more,
that *'by the mouth of two or three witnesses every word
may be established.'* And if he refuses to hear them,
tell *it* to the church. But if he refuses even to hear
the church, let him be to you like a heathen and a
tax collector" (Matt. 18:15–17).

Goal: Reconciliation and Restoration

Now all things *are* of God, who has reconciled us to
Himself through Jesus Christ, and has given us the

ministry of reconciliation, that is, that God was in Christ reconciling the world to Himself, not imputing their trespasses to them, and has committed to us the word of reconciliation. Therefore we are ambassadors for Christ, as though God were pleading through us: we implore *you* on Christ's behalf, be reconciled to God (2 Cor. 5:18–20).

Brethren, if a man is overtaken in any trespass, you who *are* spiritual restore such a one in a spirit of gentleness, considering yourself lest you also be tempted (Gal. 6:1).

= 8 =

Love

The greatest of all human qualities is love, because it is an expression of the very essence of God. His is an unconditional love that loves us in spite of ourselves. The Bible tells us that God loved us "while we were still sinners" (Rom. 5:8). His love was expressed in sending Christ to the cross to pay the penalty of sin for us.

Every discussion of love in a Christian context must be viewed, therefore, in light of Christ's love for us. How can we who are loved so much fail to love others? Love is the most natural expression of the Christian life. Those who cannot love have reason to question the reality of their salvation, for love is the fruit of the Spirit of God (see Galatians 5:22).

Learning to love is a lifelong process of growth and maturity. Most of us love those that love us. Initially our love is often narrow and self-centered. Eventually it expands toward family, friends, neighbors and ultimately even to our enemies. It is the maturing of our love that outwardly expresses the reality of Christ to others.

The Bible identifies several areas of responsibility in our expressions of love: 1) God, 2) Self, 3) Spouse, 4) Children, 5) Neighbors, 6) Strangers, 7) Enemies. It may take you a lifetime to work on these responsibilities, but at least you have a lifetime to work on them. As you allow God to control your life, His love will be personified in you. The sooner you get started, the better you will feel.

Love Is an Expression of the Character of God

God Is the Source of Love

Beloved, let us love one another, for love is of God; and everyone who loves is born of God and knows God (1 John 4:7).

But the fruit of the Spirit is love, joy, peace, longsuffering, kindness, goodness, faithfulness, . . . (Gal. 5:22).

. . . to know the love of Christ which passes knowledge; that you may be filled with all the fullness of God (Eph. 3:19).

Love Is the Greatest Virtue

And now abide faith, hope, love, these three; but the greatest of these is love (1 Cor. 13:13).

But above all these things put on love, which is the bond of perfection (Col. 3:14).

100

Now the purpose of the commandment is love from a pure heart, *from* a good conscience, and *from* sincere faith, . . (1 Tim. 1:5).

A time to love,
And a time to hate;
A time of war,
And a time of peace (Eccles. 3:8).

God Is the Object of Our Love

God Initiates Our Love

We love Him because He first loved us (1 John 4:19).

. . . . and from Jesus Christ, the faithful witness, the firstborn from the dead, and the ruler over the kings of the earth. To Him who loved us and washed us from our sins in His own blood, . . .
(Rev. 1:5).

In this is love, not that we loved God, but that He loved us and sent His Son *to be* the propitiation for our sins (1 John 4:10).

God Receives Our Love

"You shall love the LORD your God with all your heart, with all your soul, and with all your might" (Deut. 6:5).

"And the LORD your God will circumcise your heart and the heart of your descendants, to love the LORD your God with all your heart and with all your soul, that you may live" (Deut. 30:6).

101

I will love You, O LORD, my strength.
The LORD is my rock and my fortress and my
  deliverer;
My God, my strength, in whom I will trust;
My shield and the horn of my salvation, my
  stronghold.
I will call upon the LORD, *who is worthy* to be
  praised;
So shall I be saved from my enemies (Ps. 18:1–3).

"But take diligent heed to do the commandment
and the law which Moses the servant of the LORD
commanded you, to love the LORD your God, to
walk in all His ways, to keep His commandments,
to hold fast to Him, and to serve Him with all your
heart and with all your soul. . . . Therefore take
diligent heed to yourselves, that you love the LORD
your God" (Josh. 22:5; 23:11).

Oh, love the LORD, all you His saints!
For the LORD preserves the faithful,
And fully repays the proud person.
Be of good courage,
And He shall strengthen your heart,
All you who hope in the LORD (Ps. 31:23–24).

God Loves Us

For God so loved the world that He gave His only
begotten Son, that whoever believes in Him should
not perish but have everlasting life (John 3:16).

But God, who is rich in mercy, because of His great love with which He loved us, . . . (Eph. 2:4).

Now may our LORD Jesus Christ Himself, and our God and Father, who has loved us and given *us* everlasting consolation and good hope by grace, . . . (2 Thess. 2:16).

Jesus answered and said to her, "If you knew the gift of God, and who it is who says to you, 'Give Me a drink,' you would have asked Him, and He would have given you living water" (John 4:10).

"Greater love has no one than this, than to lay down one's life for his friends" (John 15:13).

"I have been crucified with Christ; it is no longer I who live, but Christ lives in me; and the *life* which I now live in the flesh I live by faith in the Son of God, who loved me and gave Himself for me" (Gal. 2:20).

God Enables Us to Love Others

Family

Husbands, love your wives, just as Christ also loved the church and gave Himself for it, . . . So husbands ought to love their own wives as their own bodies; he who loves his wife loves himself (Eph. 5:25,28).

. . . that they admonish the young women to love their husbands, to love their children, to be discreet, chaste, homemakers, good, obedient to their own husbands, that the word of God may not be blasphemed (Titus 2:4–5).

If someone says, "I love God," and hates his brother, he is a liar; for he who does not love his brother whom he has seen, how can he love God whom he has not seen? And this commandment we have from Him: that he who loves God *must* love his brother also (1 John 4:20–21).

Friends
A friend loves at all times,
And a brother is born for adversity (Prov. 17:17).

Beloved, if God so loved us, we also ought to love one another (1 John 4:11).

I am distressed for you, my brother Jonathan;
You have been very pleasant to me;
Your love to me was wonderful,
Surpassing the love of women (2 Sam. 1:26).

"A new commandment I give to you, that you love one another; as I have loved you, that you also love one another" (John 13:34).

He who loves his brother abides in the light, and there is no cause for stumbling in him (1 John 2:10).

Neighbors
"'You shall not take vengeance, nor bear any grudge against the children of your people, but you

shall love your neighbor as yourself: I *am* the LORD'"
(Lev. 19:18).

"Teacher, which *is* the great commandment in the
law?" Jesus said to him, " '*You shall love the LORD
your God with all your heart, with all your soul, and
with all your mind.*' This is *the* first and great
commandment. And *the* second *is* like it: '*You shall
love your neighbor as yourself.*' On these two
commandments hang all the Law and the
Prophets." (Matt. 22:36–40).

Strangers

"Therefore love the stranger, for you were strangers
in the land of Egypt" (Deut. 10:19).

Enemies

"You have heard that it was said, 'You shall love
your neighbor and hate your enemy.' But I say to
you, love your enemies, bless those who curse you,
do good to those who hate you, and pray for those
who spitefully use you and persecute you, . . ."
(Matt. 5:43–44).

"But I say to you who hear: Love your enemies, do
good to those who hate you, bless those who curse
you, and pray for those who spitefully use you"
(Luke 6:27–28).

*"Therefore if your enemy hungers, feed him;
If he thirsts, give him a drink;
For in so doing you will heap coals of fire on his head."*

Do not be overcome by evil, but overcome evil with good (Rom. 12:20–21).

We Are to Love the Things of God

Love His Word

Oh, how I love Your law!
It *is* my meditation all the day. . . .
Therefore I love Your commandments
More than gold, yes, than fine gold! . . .
Consider how I love Your precepts;
Revive me, O LORD, according to Your
   lovingkindness. . . .
Great peace have those who love Your law,
And nothing causes them to stumble
   (Ps. 119:97,127,159,165).

Love His Commands

And I will delight myself in Your commandments,
Which I love.
My hands also I will lift up to Your
   commandments,
Which I love,
And I will meditate on Your statutes (Ps. 119:47,48).

I will run in the way of Your commandments,
For You shall enlarge my heart (Ps. 119:32).

Also, the descendants of His servants shall inherit
   it,
And those who love His name shall dwell in it
   (Ps. 69:36).

Love Wisdom

I love those who love me,
And those who seek me diligently will find me
   (Prov. 8:17).

Happy *is* the man *who* finds wisdom,
And the man *who* gains understanding;
For her proceeds *are* better than the profit of silver,
And her gain than fine gold.
She *is* more precious than rubies,
And all the things you may desire cannot compare
   with her.
Length of days *is* in her right hand,
In her left hand riches and honor.
Her ways *are* ways of pleasantness,
And all her paths *are* peace.
She *is* a tree of life to those who take hold of her,
And happy *are all* who retain her (Prov. 3:13–18).

Love Salvation

Let all those who seek You rejoice and be glad in
   You;
Let such as love Your salvation say continually,
"The LORD be magnified!" (Ps. 40:16).

Qualities of Love

Love Never Fails

Love suffers long *and* is kind; love does not envy;
love does not parade itself, is not puffed up; does
not behave rudely, does not seek its own, is not
provoked, thinks no evil; does not rejoice in

iniquity, but rejoices in the truth; bears all things, believes all things, hopes all things, endures all things. Love never fails (1 Cor. 13:4–8).

Love Proves Our Salvation

"By this all will know that you are My disciples, if you have love for one another" (John 13:35).

We know that we have passed from death to life, because we love the brethren. He who does not love *his* brother abides in death (1 John 3:14).

Beloved, let us love one another, for love is of God; and everyone who loves is born of God and knows God. He who does not love does not know God, for God is love (1 John 4:7–8).

"For whom the LORD loves He chastens,
And scourges every son whom He receives" (Heb. 12:6).

Love Overcomes Our Fears

For God has not given us a spirit of fear, but of power and of love and of a sound mind (2 Tim. 1:7).

There is no fear in love; but perfect love casts out fear, because fear involves torment. But he who fears has not been made perfect in love (1 John 4:18).

Love Produces Obedience

"If you love Me, keep My commandments" (John 14:15).

"He who has My commandments and keeps them, it is he who loves Me. And he who loves Me will be loved by My Father, and I will love him and manifest Myself to him" (John 14:21).

"If you keep My commandments, you will abide in My love, just as I have kept My Father's commandments and abide in His love" (John 15:10).

Love Brings Prosperity

Pray for the peace of Jerusalem:
"May they prosper who love you" (Ps. 122:6).

The LORD preserves all who love Him,
But all the wicked He will destroy (Ps. 145:20).

Love Enables us to Forgive

Hatred stirs up strife,
But love covers all sins (Prov. 10:12).

He who covers a transgression seeks love,
But he who repeats a matter separates *the best of* friends (Prov. 17:9).

"Therefore I say to you, her sins, *which are* many, are forgiven, for she loved much. But to whom little is forgiven, *the same* loves little" (Luke 7:47).

Love Conquers All

Yet in all these things we are more than conquerors through Him who loved us. For I am persuaded that neither death nor life, nor angels nor principalities nor powers, nor things present nor things to come, nor height nor depth, nor any other created thing, shall be able to separate us from the love of God which is in Christ Jesus our Lord (Rom. 8:37–39).

= 9 =

Sex

The Bible has a great deal to say about sex
and addresses this basic fact of life sincerely
and straightforwardly. The Bible tells us the
purpose of sex, the proper boundaries of sex
and the key to sexual happiness and
fulfillment. In a society that is often obsessed
with sex, it is vital to understand the true
nature and purpose of this great gift of God.

Sex is the common term used today to
describe the physical union of men and
women. The Bible clearly states that this union
is undefiled and blessed of God (see Hebrews
13:4). It is the natural physical expression of
human love. But the Bible also emphasizes that
sexual love belongs within the boundaries of
marriage.

The Scripture warns against the
destructiveness of infidelity and urges marital
fidelity as the path that leads to love,
happiness and security. Keeping the marriage
bond is essential in promoting strong and
stable families. Fidelity assures each partner of
the loyalty and commitment of the other.

Unfortunately sex is often misunderstood by Christians. Before marriage, we are told, "Wait, don't do it." After marriage, we are told, "Go ahead, it's all right." If we are not careful, we can spend so much energy being on guard against temptation that we neglect each other. Such neglect is called "defrauding," and married couples are urged not to neglect one another (see 1 Corinthians 7:2–5). Sexual happiness and fulfillment are God's intention for every married couple.

Purpose of Sex

Procreation

So God created man in His *own* image; in the image of God He created him; male and female He created them. Then God blessed them, and God said to them, "Be fruitful and multiply; fill the earth and subdue it; have dominion over the fish of the sea, over the birds of the air, and over every living thing that moves on the earth" (Gen. 1:27–28).

Now Adam knew Eve his wife, and she conceived and bore Cain, and said, "I have gotten a man from the LORD" (Gen. 4:1).

And Adam lived one hundred and thirty years, and begot *a son* in his own likeness, after his image, and named him Seth. After he begot Seth, the days of Adam were eight hundred years; and he begot sons and daughters (Gen. 5:3–4).

So God blessed Noah and his sons, and said to them: "Be fruitful and multiply and fill the earth" (Gen. 9:1).

Unity

Therefore a man shall leave his father and mother and be joined to his wife, and they shall become one flesh. And they were both naked, the man and his wife, and were not ashamed (Gen. 2:24–25).

My beloved *is* mine, and I *am* his.
He feeds *his flock* among the lilies
  (Song of Sol. 2:16).

I *am* my beloved's,
And my beloved *is* mine.
He feeds *his flock* among the lilies (Song of Sol. 6:3).

I *am* my beloved's,
And his desire *is* toward me (Song of Sol. 7:10).

Fulfillment

Marriage *is* honorable among all, and the bed undefiled; but fornicators and adulterers God will judge (Heb. 13:4).

. . . but if they cannot exercise self-control, let them marry. For it is better to marry than to burn *with passion* (1 Cor. 7:9).

Pleasure

Drink water from your own cistern,
And running water from your own well.
Should your fountains be dispersed abroad,

113

Streams of water in the streets?
Let them be only your own,
And not for strangers with you.
Let your fountain be blessed,
And rejoice with the wife of your youth.
As a loving deer and a graceful doe,
Let her breasts satisfy you at all times;
And always be enraptured with her love
   (Prov. 5:15–19).

My beloved *is* white and ruddy,
Chief among ten thousand.
His head *is like* the finest gold;
His locks *are* wavy,
And black as a raven.
His eyes *are* like doves
By the rivers of waters,
Washed with milk,
And fitly set.
His cheeks *are* like a bed of spices,
Like banks of scented herbs.
His lips *are* lilies,
Dripping liquid myrrh.
His hands *are* rods of gold
Set with beryl.
His body *is* carved ivory
Inlaid *with* sapphires.
His legs *are* pillars of marble
Set on bases of fine gold.
His countenance *is* like Lebanon,
Excellent as the cedars.

His mouth *is* most sweet,
Yes, he *is* altogether lovely.
This *is* my beloved,
And this *is* my friend,
O daughters of Jerusalem! (Song of Sol. 5:10–16).

How beautiful are your feet in sandals,
O prince's daughter!
The curves of your thighs *are* like jewels,
The work of the hands of a skillful workman.
Your naval *is* a rounded goblet
Which lacks no blended beverage.
Your waist *is* a heap of wheat
Set about with lilies.
Your two breasts *are* like two fawns,
Twins of a gazelle.
Your neck *is* like an ivory tower,
Your eyes *like* the pools in Heshbon
By the gate of Bath Rabbim.
Your nose *is* like the tower of Lebanon
Which looks toward Damascus.
Your head *crowns* you like *Mount* Carmel,
And the hair of your head *is* like purple;
The king *is* held captive by *its* tresses.
How fair and how pleasant you are,
O love, with your delights!
This stature of yours is like a palm tree,
And your breasts *like* its clusters.
I said, "I will go up to the palm tree,
I will take hold of its branches."
Let now your breasts be like clusters of the vine,

The fragrance of your breath like apples,
And the roof of your mouth like the best wine.
The wine goes *down* smoothly for my beloved,
Moving gently the lips of sleepers.
I *am* my beloved's,
And his desire *is* toward me (Song of Sol. 7:1–10).

Sexual Responsibility Outside of Marriage
Commit Your Body to God

I beseech you therefore, brethren, by the mercies of God, that you present your bodies a living sacrifice, holy, acceptable to God, *which is* your reasonable service. And do not be conformed to this world, but be transformed by the renewing of your mind, that you may prove what *is* that good and acceptable and perfect will of God (Rom. 12:1–2).

And do not present your members *as* instruments of unrighteousness to sin, but present yourselves to God as being alive from the dead, and your members *as* instruments of righteousness to God (Rom. 6:13).

I speak in human *terms* because of the weakness of your flesh. For just as you presented your members *as* slaves of uncleanness, and of lawlessness *leading* to *more* lawlessness, so now present your members *as* slaves *of* righteousness for holiness. For when you were slaves of sin, you were free in regard to righteousness (1 Cor. 6:19–20).

Establish Standards and Boundaries

For this is the will of God, your sanctification: that you should abstain from sexual immorality; that each of you should know how to possess his own vessel in sanctification and honor, not in passion of lust, like the Gentiles who do not know God; that no one should take advantage of and defraud his brother in this matter, because the Lord *is* the avenger of all such, as we also forewarned you and testified. For God did not call us to uncleanness, but in holiness (1 Thess. 4:3–7).

Flee also youthful lusts; but pursue righteousness, faith, love, peace with those who call on the Lord out of a pure heart (2 Tim. 2:22).

Where do wars and fights *come* from among you? Do *they* not *come* from your *desires for* pleasure that war in your members? You lust and do not have. You murder and covet and cannot obtain. You fight and war. Yet you do not have because you do not ask. You ask and do not receive, because you ask amiss, that you may spend *it* on your pleasures. Adulterers and adulteresses! Do you not know that friendship with the world is enmity with God? Whoever therefore wants to be a friend of the world makes himself enemy of God (James 4:1–4).

Beloved, I beg *you* as sojourners and pilgrims, abstain from fleshly lusts which war against the soul, having your conduct honorable among the Gentiles, that when they speak against you as evildoers, they may, by *your* good works which they observe, glorify God in the day of visitation (1 Peter 2:11–12).

Control Eyes and Habits

. . . having eyes full of adultery and that cannot cease from sin, beguiling unstable souls. *They have* a heart trained in covetous practices, *and are* accursed children. They have forsaken the right way and gone astray, following the way of Balaam the *son* of Beor, who loved the wages of unrighteousness; . . . (2 Peter 2:14–15).

But fornication and all uncleanness or covetousness, let it not even be named among you, as is fitting for saints; neither filthiness, nor foolish talking, nor coarse jesting, which are not fitting, but rather giving of thanks (Eph. 5:3–4).

Sexual Responsibility Within Marriage

Be Consistent: Do Not Defraud

Nevertheless, because of sexual immorality, let each man have his own wife, and let each woman have her own husband. Let the husband render to his wife the affection due her, and likewise also the wife to her husband. The wife does not have authority over her own body, but the husband *does*. And likewise the husband does not have authority over his own body, but the wife *does*. Do not deprive one another except with consent for a time, that you may give yourselves to fasting and prayer; and come together again so that Satan does not tempt you because of your lack of self-control (1 Cor. 7:2–5).

Be Loving: Please Your Partner

There is a difference between a wife and a virgin. The unmarried woman cares about the things of the Lord, that she may be holy both in body and in spirit. But she who is married cares about the things of the world—how she may please *her* husband (1 Cor. 7:34).

Be Warm: Give Yourself

Set me as a seal upon your heart,
As a seal upon your arm;
For love *is as* strong as death,
Jealousy *as* cruel as the grave;
Its flames *are* flames of fire,
A most vehement flame.
Many waters cannot quench love.
Nor can the floods drown it.
If a man would give for love
All the wealth of his house,
It would be utterly despised (Song of Sol. 8:6–7).

Sexual Happiness Is Based upon Genuine Love

Love Is the Greatest Emotion

And now abide faith, hope, love, these three; but the greatest of these *is* love (1 Cor. 13:13).

For God has not given us a spirit of fear, but of power and of love and of a sound mind (2 Tim. 1:7).

There is no fear in love; but perfect love casts out fear, because fear involves torment. But he who fears has not been made perfect in love (1 John 4:18).

But above all these things put on love, which is the bond of perfection (Col. 3:14).

Love Expresses the Character of God

Though I speak with the tongues of men and of angels, but have not love, I have become *as* sounding brass or a clanging cymbal. And though I have *the gift of* prophecy, and understand all mysteries and all knowledge, and though I have all faith, so that I could remove mountains, but have not love, I am nothing (1 Cor. 13:1–2).

. . . to know the love of Christ which passes knowledge; that you may be filled with all the fullness of God (Eph. 3:19).

Beloved, let us love one another, for love is of God; and everyone who loves is born of God and knows God (1 John 4:7).

And this I pray, that your love may abound still more and more in knowledge and all discernment, that you may approve the things that are excellent, that you may be sincere and without offense till the day of Christ, being filled with the fruits of righteousness which *are* by Jesus Christ, to the glory and praise of God (Phil. 1:9–11).

Love Reassures Your Partner of Your Devotion
"By this all will know that you are My disciples, if you have love for one another" (John 13:35).

. . . that they admonish the young women to love their husbands, to love their children, to be discreet, chaste, homemakers, good, obedient to their own husbands, that the word of God may not be blasphemed (Titus 2:4–5).

Now the purpose of the commandment is love from a pure heart, *from* a good conscience, and *from* sincere faith, . . . (1 Tim. 1:5).

Husbands, love your wives, just as Christ also loved the church and gave Himself for it, . . . (Eph. 5:25).

Therefore, as *the* elect of God, holy and beloved, put on tender mercies, kindness, humbleness of mind, meekness, longsuffering; bearing with one another, and forgiving one another, if anyone has a complaint against another; even as Christ forgave you, so you also *must do.* But above all these things put on love, which is the bond of perfection (Col. 3:12–14).

═10═

Adultery

Jesus once called the people of His day a "wicked and adulterous generation" (Matt. 16:4). He accused them of being ashamed of Him and announced that He would be ashamed of them at His second coming (see Mark 8:38). How much more could He accuse our generation today!

Adultery is a violation of the covenant of marriage. It involves willful sexual immorality with a person to whom one is not married. It begins in the heart, is expressed in the eyes and results in a physical act of sexual intercourse. It is a sin against God and one's own marriage. It has disastrous personal consequences that are often irreparable and irrecoverable.

The Bible is filled with warnings against adultery, including detailed descriptions of how the process works. In every case, adultery is severely condemned as a violation of the marriage vow, a threat to the family and an erosion of society itself.

Fidelity to the marriage vow is commanded

in Scripture as cement that holds marriages together, families together and keeps society on course. If there were ever a time that such urgings and warnings needed to be heard, it is now.

Adultery Is a Sin

A Sin Against God

"You shall not commit adultery" (Exod. 20:14).

"*There is* no one greater in this house than I, nor has he kept back anything from me but you, because you *are* his wife. How then can I do this great wickedness, and sin against God?" (Gen. 39:9).

You who say, "Do not commit adultery," do you commit adultery? You who abhor idols, do you rob temples? You who make your boast in the law, do you dishonor God through breaking the law? For *"The name of God is blasphemed among the Gentiles because of you,"* as it is written (Rom. 2:22–24).

Do you not know that the unrighteous will not inherit the kingdom of God? Do not be deceived. Neither fornicators, nor idolators, nor adulterers, nor homosexuals, nor sodomites, . . . (1 Cor. 6:9).

A Sin Against the Holy Spirit

Do you not know that your bodies are members of Christ? Shall I then take the members of Christ and make *them* members of a harlot? Certainly not! Or

123

do you not know that he who is joined to a harlot is one body *with her*? For *"The two,"* He says, *"shall become one flesh."* But he who is joined to the Lord is one spirit *with Him*. Flee sexual immorality. Every sin that a man does is outside the body, but he who commits sexual immorality sins against his own body. Or do you not know that your body is the temple of the Holy Spirit *who is* in you, whom you have from God, and you are not your own? For you were bought at a price; therefore glorify God in your body and in your spirit, which are God's (1 Cor. 6:15–20).

A Sin Against One's Partner

To deliver you from the immoral woman,
From the seductress *who* flatters with her words,
Who forsakes the companion of her youth,
And forgets the covenant of her God.
For her house leads down to death,
And her paths to the dead;
None who go to her return,
Nor do they regain the paths of life—
   (Prov. 2:16–19).

Let your fountain be blessed,
And rejoice with the wife of your youth.
As a loving deer and a graceful doe,
Let her breasts satisfy you at all times;
And always be enraptured with her love.
For why should you, my son, be enraptured by an
   immoral woman,

124

And be embraced in the arms of a seductress?
For the ways of man *are* before the eyes of the
   LORD,
And He ponders all his paths (Prov. 5:18–21).

Say to wisdom, "You *are* my sister,"
And call understanding *your* nearest kin,
That they may keep you from the immoral woman,
From the seductress *who* flatters with her words
   (Prov. 7:4–5).

An excellent wife *is* the crown of her husband,
But she who causes shame *is* like rottenness in his
   bones (Prov. 12:4).

Who can find a virtuous wife?
For her worth *is* far above rubies.
The heart of her husband safely trusts her;
So he will have no lack of gain (Prov. 31:10–11).

A Sin Against Oneself

Flee sexual immorality. Every sin that a man does is
outside the body, but he who commits sexual
immorality sins against his own body (1 Cor. 6:18).

"But those things which proceed out of the mouth
come from the heart, and they defile a man. For
out of the heart proceed evil thoughts, murders,
adulteries, fornications, thefts, false witness,
blasphemies. These are *the things* which defile a
man, . . ." (Matt. 15:18–20).

But I say to you that whoever looks at a woman to lust for her has already committed adultery with her in his heart" (Matt. 5:28).

Therefore God also gave them up to uncleanness, in the lusts of their hearts, to dishonor their bodies among themselves, who exchanged the truth of God for the lie, and worshiped and served the creature rather than the Creator, who is blessed forever. Amen (Rom. 1:24–25).

. . . being filled with all unrighteousness, sexual immorality, wickedness, covetousness, maliciousness; full of envy, murder, strife, deceit, evil-mindedness; *they are* whisperers, backbiters, haters of God, violent, proud, boasters, inventors of evil things, disobedient to parents, undiscerning, untrustworthy, unloving, unforgiving, unmerciful; who, knowing the righteous judgment of God, that those who practice such things are worthy of death, not only do the same but also approve of those who practice them (Rom. 1:29–32).

A Sin Against the Church

But now I have written to you not to keep company with anyone named a brother, who is a fornicator, or covetous, or an idolater, or a reviler, or a drunkard, or an extortioner—not even to eat with such a person (1 Cor. 5:11).

But fornication and all uncleanness or covetousness, let it not even be named among you, as is fitting for

saints; neither filthiness, nor foolish talking, nor
coarse jesting, which are not fitting, but rather
giving of thanks. For this you know, that no
fornicator, unclean person, nor covetous man, who
is an idolater, has any inheritance in the kingdom of
Christ and God. Let no one deceive you with
empty words, for because of these things the wrath
of God comes upon the sons of disobedience.
Therefore do not be partakers with them
(Eph. 5:3–7).

Consequences of Adultery

Guilt

Can one walk on hot coals,
And his feet not be seared?
So *is* he who goes in to his neighbor's wife;
Whoever touches her shall not be innocent
    (Prov. 6:28–29).

Dishonor

Whoever commits adultery with a woman lacks
    understanding;
He *who* does so destroys his own soul.
Wounds and dishonor he will get,
And his reproach will not be wiped away
    (Prov. 6:32–33).

Shame

"*By* swearing and lying,
Killing and stealing and committing adultery,
They break all restraint,

With bloodshed after bloodshed.
My people are destroyed for lack of knowledge.
Because you have rejected knowledge,
I also will reject you from being priest for Me;
Because you have forgotten the law of your God,
I also will forget your children.
The more they increased,
The more they sinned against Me;
I will change their glory into shame" (Hos. 4:2,6–7).

Poverty

Do not lust after her beauty in your heart,
Nor let her allure you with her eyelids.
For by means of a harlot
A man is reduced to a crust of bread;
And an adulteress will prey upon his precious life
   (Prov. 6:25–26).

Remove your way far from her,
And do not go near the door of her house,
Lest you give your honor to others,
And your years to the cruel one;
Lest aliens be filled with your wealth, . . .
(Prov. 5:8–10).

Bitterness

For the lips of an immoral woman drip honey,
And her mouth *is* smoother than oil;
But in the end she is bitter as wormwood,
Sharp as a two-edged sword.
Her feet go down to death,
Her steps lay hold of hell (Prov. 5:3–5).

128

Destruction

A foolish woman is clamorous;
She is simple, and knows nothing.
For she sits at the door of her house,
On a seat *by* the highest places of the city,
To call to those who pass by,
Who go straight on their way:
"Whoever *is* simple, let him turn in here";
And *as for* him who lacks understanding, she says
 to him,
"Stolen water is sweet,
And bread *eaten* in secret is pleasant."
But he does not know that the dead *are* there,
That her guests *are* in the depths of hell
 (Prov. 9:13–18).

And there a woman met him,
With the attire of a harlot, and a crafty heart.
She *was* loud and rebellious,
Her feet would not stay at home.
At times *she was* outside, at times in the open
 square,
Lurking at every corner.
So she caught him and kissed him;
With an impudent face she said to him:
"*I have* peace offerings with me;
Today I have paid my vows.
So I came out to meet you,
Diligently to seek your face,
And I have found you.
I have spread my bed with tapestry,

Colored coverings of Egyptian linen.
I have perfumed my bed
With myrrh, aloes, and cinnamon.
Come, let us take our fill of love until morning;
Let us delight ourselves with love.
For my husband *is* not at home;
He has gone on a long journey;
He has taken a bag of money with him,
And will come home on the appointed day."
With her enticing speech she caused him to yield,
With her flattering lips she seduced him.
Immediately he went after her, as an ox goes to the
     slaughter,
Or as a fool to the correction of the stocks,
Till an arrow struck his liver.
As a bird hastens to the snare,
He did not know it *would take* his life.
Now therefore, listen to me, *my* children;
Pay attention to the words of my mouth:
Do not let your heart turn aside to her ways,
Do not stray into her paths;
For she has cast down many wounded,
And all who were slain by her were strong *men.*
Her house *is* the way to hell,
Descending to the chambers of death
     (Prov. 7:10–27).

Can Adultery Be Forgiven?

Adultery Is Not the Unpardonable Sin

"Therefore I say to you, every sin and blasphemy will be forgiven men, but the blasphemy *against* the Spirit will not be forgiven men. Anyone who speaks a word against the Son of Man, it will be forgiven him; but whoever speaks against the Holy Spirit, it will not be forgiven him, either in this age or in the *age* to come" (Matt. 12:31–32).

All Other Sin Can Be Forgiven

If we confess our sins, He is faithful and just to forgive us *our* sins and to cleanse us from all unrighteousness (1 John 1:9).

Therefore, if anyone *is* in Christ, *he is* a new creation; old things have passed away; behold, all things have become new. Now all things *are* of God, who has reconciled us to Himself through Jesus Christ, and has given us the ministry of reconciliation, that is, that God was in Christ reconciling the world to Himself, not imputing their trespasses to them, and has committed to us the word of reconciliation. Therefore we are ambassadors for Christ, as though God were pleading through us: we implore *you* on Christ's behalf, be reconciled to God. For He made Him who knew no sin *to be* sin for us, that we might become the righteousness of God in Him (2 Cor. 5:17–21).

Jesus Offered Forgiveness

Then the scribes and Pharisees brought to Him a woman caught in adultery. And when they had set her in the midst, they said to Him, "Teacher, this woman was caught in adultery, in the very act. Now Moses, in the law, commanded us that such should be stoned. But what do You say?" This they said, testing Him, that they might have *something* of which to accuse Him. But Jesus stooped down and wrote on the ground with *His* finger, as though He did not hear. So when they continued asking Him, He raised Himself up and said to them, "He who is without sin among you, let him throw a stone at her first." And again He stooped down and wrote on the ground. Then those who heard *it*, being convicted by *their* conscience, went out one by one, beginning with the oldest *even* to the last. And Jesus was left alone, and the woman standing in the midst. When Jesus had raised Himself up and saw no one but the woman, He said to her, "Woman, where are those accusers of yours? Has no one condemned you?" She said, "No one, Lord." And Jesus said to her, "Neither do I condemn you; go and sin no more" (John 8:3–11).

Paul Urged Forgiveness

This punishment which *was inflicted* by the majority *is* sufficient for such a man, so that, on the contrary, you *ought* rather to forgive and comfort *him*, lest perhaps such a one be swallowed up with too much sorrow. Therefore I urge you to reaffirm *your* love to him (2 Cor. 2:6–8).

Forgiveness Is Conditioned by Repentance
"Take heed to yourselves. If your brother sins against you, rebuke him; and if he repents, forgive him" (Luke 17:3).

"Moreover if your brother sins against you, go and tell him his fault between you and him alone. If he hears you, you have gained your brother. But if he will not hear *you*, take with you one or two more, that *'by the mouth of two or three witnesses every word may be established.'* And if he refuses to hear them, tell *it* to the church. But if he refuses even to hear the church, let him be to you like a heathen and a tax collector" (Matt. 18:15–17).

He who covers his sins will not prosper,
But whoever confesses and forsakes *them* will have
   mercy (Prov. 28:13).

═ 11 ═

Temptation

The temptation to sin is a constant struggle in our lives. It is especially dangerous to healthy marriages. In a time when adultery and infidelity are at an all time high, men and women need to learn how to resist temptation more than ever.

The Bible tells us that temptation is both external and internal. We may be tempted by people or things, but ultimately the real battle is within ourselves (see James 1:14). We must learn to control our physical desires by the power of the Spirit.

Temptation may confront you directly or indirectly. Either way, it must be faced for what it is. When Jesus was tempted by Satan in the wilderness, He responded with the powerful word of God and came away victorious.

We find several keys to victory over temptation in the Scripture. These include committing your body, renewing your mind and resisting the devil. Conquering temptation is not an easy process. It takes time, diligence, discipline and self-sacrifice. But the results are worth the effort. The more you resist now, the more you will be able to resist in the future. Today's self-discipline is the key to tomorrow's success.

Life is filled with traps and snares. Be on the lookout. Keep your eye on the sources of temptation and stay away from them. Follow the biblical guidelines: "make no provision for the flesh" (Rom. 13:14); "resist the devil" (James 4:7); and "take the way of escape" (1 Cor. 10:13).

Commit Your Body to the Lord

Be Conformed to His Will

I beseech you therefore, brethren, by the mercies of God, that you present your bodies a living sacrifice, holy, acceptable to God, *which is* your reasonable service. And do not be conformed to this world, but be transformed by the renewing of your mind, that you may prove what *is* that good and acceptable and perfect will of God (Rom. 12:1–2).

Die to Sinful Desires

. . . knowing this, that our old man was crucified with *Him*, that the body of sin might be done away with, that we should no longer be slaves of sin. . . . Likewise you also, reckon yourselves to be dead indeed to sin, but alive to God in Christ Jesus our Lord (Rom. 6:6,11).

Yield Yourself to God

Therefore do not let sin reign in your mortal body, that you should obey it in its lusts. And do not present your members *as* instruments of unrighteousness to sin, but present yourselves to God as being alive from the dead, and your members *as* instruments of righteousness to God (Rom. 6:12–13).

Die Daily to Selfish Desires

Then He said to *them* all, "If anyone desires to come after Me, let him deny himself, and take up his cross daily, and follow Me" (Luke 9:23).

"And he who does not take his cross and follow after Me is not worthy of Me" (Matt. 10:38).

Then Jesus said to His disciples, "If anyone desires to come after Me, let him deny himself, and take up his cross, and follow Me" (Matt. 16:24).

Expect a Struggle

For we know that the law is spiritual, but I am carnal, sold under sin. For what I am doing, I do not understand. For what I will to do, that I do not practice; but what I hate, that I do. If, then, I do what I will not to do, I agree with the law that *it is* good. But now, *it is* no longer I who do it, but sin that dwells in me. For I know that in me (that is, in my flesh) nothing good dwells; for to will is present with me, but *how* to perform what is good I do not find (Rom. 7:14–18).

Your Body Belongs to God

Do you not know that your bodies are members of Christ? Shall I then take the members of Christ and make *them* members of a harlot? Certainly not! Or do you not know that he who is joined to a harlot is one body *with her*? For *"The two,"* He says, *"shall become one flesh."* But he who is joined to the Lord is one spirit *with Him.* Flee sexual immorality. Every sin that a man does is outside the body, but he who commits sexual immorality sins against his own body. Or do you not know that your body is the temple of the Holy Spirit *who is* in you, whom you have from God, and you are not your own? For you were bought at a price; therefore glorify God in your body and in your spirit, which are God's (1 Cor. 6:15–20).

Cleanse Your Mind

Lust Begins in the Mind

"But I say to you that whoever looks at a woman to lust for her has already committed adultery with her in his heart" (Matt. 5:28).

Carnal Minds Are Controlled by the Flesh

For to be carnally minded *is* death, but to be spiritually minded *is* life and peace. Because the carnal mind *is* enmity against God; for it is not subject to the law of God, nor indeed can be. So then, those who are in the flesh cannot please God (Rom. 8:6–8).

137

Temptation Comes From Within

Let no one say when he is tempted, "I am tempted
by God"; for God cannot be tempted by evil, nor
does He Himself tempt anyone. But each one is
tempted when he is drawn away by his own desires
and enticed. Then, when desire has conceived, it
gives birth to sin; and sin, when it is full-grown,
brings forth death (James 1:13–15).

For the flesh lusts against the Spirit, and the Spirit
against the flesh; and these are contrary to one
another, so that you do not do the things that you
wish (Gal. 5:17).

Meditate on Good Things

Nevertheless she will be saved in childbearing if
they continue in faith, love, and holiness, with self-
control (1 Tim. 2:15).

Finally, brethren, whatever things are true,
whatever things *are* noble, whatever things *are* just,
whatever things *are* pure, whatever things *are*
lovely, whatever things *are* of good report, if *there is*
any virtue and if *there is* anything praiseworthy—
meditate on these things (Phil. 4:8).

Watch Your Friends

Temptation Comes From Others

My son, if sinners entice you,
Do not consent (Prov. 1:10).

A violent man entices his neighbor,
And leads him in a way *that is* not good
(Prov. 16:29).

"Watch and pray, lest you enter into temptation.
The spirit truly *is* ready, but the flesh *is* weak"
(Mark 14:38).

You therefore, beloved, since you know *these things*
beforehand, beware lest you also fall from your
own steadfastness, being led away with the error of
the wicked; . . . (2 Pet. 3:17).

That they may keep you from the immoral woman,
From the seductress *who* flatters with her words
(Prov. 7:5).

Now this I say lest anyone should deceive you with
persuasive words (Col. 2:4).

Temptation Usually Seems Innocent at First

Now the serpent was more cunning than any beast
of the field which the LORD God had made. And he
said to the woman, "Has God indeed said, 'You
shall not eat of every tree of the garden'?" And the
woman said to the serpent, "We may eat the fruit of
the trees of the garden; but of the fruit of the tree
which *is* in the midst of the garden, God has said,
'You shall not eat it, nor shall you touch it, lest you
die.'" And the serpent said to the woman, "You
will not surely die" (Gen. 3:1–4).

139

Now afterward it happened that he loved a woman in the Valley of Sorek, whose name *was* Delilah. And the lords of the Philistines came up to her and said to her, "Entice him, and find out where his great strength *lies*, and by what *means* we may overpower him, that we may bind him to afflict him; and every one of us will give you eleven hundred *pieces* of silver" (Judg. 16:4–5).

Resist the Devil

He Must Be Resisted

Then Jesus was led up by the Spirit into the wilderness to be tempted by the devil. And when He had fasted forty days and forty nights, afterward He was hungry. Now when the tempter came to Him, he said, "If You are the Son of God, command that these stones become bread." But He answered and said, "It is written, *'Man shall not live by bread alone, but by every word that proceeds from the mouth of God.'"* Then the devil took Him up into the holy city, set Him on the pinnacle of the temple, and said to Him, "If You are the Son of God, throw Yourself down. For it is written:

'He shall give His angels charge concerning You,'

and,

*'In their hands they shall bear you up,
Lest you dash your foot against a stone.'"*

Jesus said to him, "It is written again, *'You shall not tempt the LORD your God.'*" Again, the devil took Him up on an exceedingly high mountain, and showed Him all the kingdoms of the world and their glory. And he said to Him, "All these things I will give You if You will fall down and worship me." Then Jesus said to him, "Away with you, Satan! For it is written, *'You shall worship the LORD your God, and Him only you shall serve.'*" Then the devil left Him, and behold, angels came and ministered to Him (Matt. 4:1–11).

Therefore submit to God. Resist the devil and he will flee from you (James 4:7).

Now the Spirit expressly says that in latter times some will depart from the faith, giving heed to deceiving spirits and doctrines of demons, . . . (1 Tim. 4:1).

Be sober, be vigilant; because your adversary the devil walks about like a roaring lion, seeking whom he may devour. Resist him, steadfast in the faith, knowing that the same sufferings are experienced by your brotherhood in the world (1 Pet. 5:8–9).

True Repentance Is Essential
But He gives more grace. Therefore He says:

> "God resists the proud,
> But gives grace to the humble."

Therefore submit to God. Resist the devil and he will flee from you. Draw near to God and He will draw near to you. Cleanse *your* hands, *you* sinners; and purify *your* hearts, *you* doubleminded. Lament and mourn and weep! Let your laughter be turned to mourning and *your* joy to gloom. Humble yourselves in the sight of the Lord, and He will lift you up (James 4:6–10).

Oh, taste and see that the LORD is good,
Blessed *is* the man *who* trusts in Him! (Ps. 34:8).

"But if a wicked man turns from all his sins which he has committed, keeps all My statutes, and does what is lawful and right, he shall surely live; he shall not die" (Ezek. 18:21).

. . . and saying, "Repent, for the kingdom of heaven is at hand!" (Matt. 3:2).

When Jesus heard *it*, He said to them, "Those who are well have no need of a physician, but those who are sick. I did not come to call *the* righteous, but sinners, to repentance" (Mark 2:17).

"Therefore bear fruits worthy of repentance, and do not begin to say to yourselves, 'We have Abraham as *our* father.' For I say to you that God is able to raise up children to Abraham from these stones" (Luke 3:8).

"I say to you that likewise there will be more joy in heaven over one sinner who repents than over ninety-nine just persons who need no repentance" (Luke 15:7).

". . . and that repentance and remission of sins should be preached in His name to all nations, beginning at Jerusalem" (Luke 24:47).

"Remember therefore from where you have fallen; repent and do the first works, or else I will come to you quickly and remove your lampstand from its place—unless you repent" (Rev. 2:5).

Flee from Lust

Make No Provision for the Flesh

Let us walk properly, as in the day, not in revelry and drunkenness, not in licentiousness and lewdness, not in strife and envy. But put on the Lord Jesus Christ, and make no provision for the flesh, to *fulfill its* lusts (Rom. 13:13–14).

Therefore let us not judge one another anymore, but rather resolve this, not to put a stumbling block or a cause to fall in *our* brother's way (Rom. 14:13).

Run Away from Temptation

Flee also youthful lusts; but pursue righteousness, faith, love, peace with those who call on the Lord out of a pure heart (2 Tim. 2:22).

No temptation has overtaken you except such as is common to man; but God *is* faithful, who will not allow you to be tempted beyond what you are able, but with the temptation will also make the way of escape, that you may be able to bear *it* (1 Cor. 10:13).

Claim God's Promises

. . . by which have been given to us exceedingly great and precious promises, that through these you may be partakers of the divine nature, having escaped the corruption *that is* in the world through lust (2 Pet. 1:4).

Blessed *is* the man who endures temptation; for when he has been proved, he will receive the crown of life which the Lord has promised to those who love Him (James 1:12).

Identify the Sources of Temptation

Evil Desires

Now these things became our examples, to the intent that we should not lust after evil things as they also lusted (1 Cor. 10:6).

Do not love the world or the things in the world. If anyone loves the world, the love of the Father is not in him. For all that *is* in the world—the lust of the flesh, the lust of the eyes, and the pride of life—is not of the Father but is of the world. And the world is passing away, and the lust of it; but he who does the will of God abides forever (1 John 2:15–17).

Take the Way of Escape

No temptation has overtaken you except such as is common to man; but God *is* faithful, who will not allow you to be tempted beyond what you are able, but with the temptation will also make the way of escape, that you may be able to bear *it* (1 Cor. 10:13).

$$=== 12 ===$$

Relationships

Getting along with people has never been easy. Sometimes it takes all the love we can muster to be at peace with those around us. Yet the heart of the Christian gospel is that of a changed relationship to Christ and others. Because He lives within us, we are able to love, accept and forgive others. He is the key to successful personal relationships.

The matters of human relations and public relations have been relegated to whole departments in most businesses. Yet in our personal relationships with others, most of us struggle along simply hoping things will get better. But the truth is that they will only get better when we make them better.

In reality, getting along with others, either inside or outside the family, depends upon our manifestation of the fruits of the Spirit: love, joy, peace, patience, gentleness, goodness, faith, meekness and self-control. Each of these qualities is essential in effective personal relationships. They balance our human weaknesses with the character qualities of God.

Relationships are intended to be one of God's blessings in our lives. But all too often they become a source of heartache and despair. God's plan is to enable us to get along with each other as brothers and sisters in His family. Loving, forgiving and understanding each other is all part of that process.

Relationships within the Family

Husbands

Husbands, love your wives, just as Christ also loved the church and gave Himself for it. . . . (Eph. 5:25).

Husbands, love your wives and do not be bitter toward them (Col. 3:19).

Likewise *you* husbands, dwell with *them* with understanding, giving honor to the wife, as to the weaker vessel, and as *being* heirs together of the grace of life, that your prayers may not be hindered (1 Pet. 3:7).

Wives

Wives, submit to your own husbands, as to the Lord. For the husband is head of the wife, as also Christ is head of the church; and He is the Savior of the body. Therefore, just as the church is subject to Christ, so *let* the wives *be* to their own husbands in everything (Eph. 5:22–24).

Wives, submit to your own husbands, as is fitting in the Lord (Col. 3:18).

. . . the older women likewise, that they be reverent in behavior, not slanderers, not given to much wine, teachers of good things—that they admonish the young women to love their husbands, to love their children, to be discreet, chaste, homemakers, good, obedient to their own husbands, that the word of God may not be blasphemed (Titus 2:3–5).

Parents

"Honor your father and mother," which is the first commandment with promise: *"that it may be well with you and you may live long on the earth"* (Eph. 6:2–3).

"For this reason a man shall leave his father and mother and be joined to his wife, and the two shall become one flesh" (Eph. 5:31).

And you, fathers, do not provoke your children to wrath, but bring them up in the training and admonition of the Lord (Eph. 6:4).

A wise son *heeds* his father's instruction,
But a scoffer does not listen to rebuke (Prov. 13:1).

Train up a child in the way he should go,
And when he is old he will not depart from it
   (Prov. 22:6).

Relationships

Children

Children, obey your parents in the Lord, for this is right (Eph. 6:1).

. . . one who rules his own house well, having *his* children in submission with all reverence (for if a man does not know how to rule his own house, how will he take care of the church of God?); . . . (1 Tim. 3:4–5).

Foolishness *is* bound up in the heart of a child,
But the rod of correction will drive it far from him
  (Prov. 22:15).

Then they brought young children to Him, that He might touch them; but the disciples rebuked those who brought *them*. But when Jesus saw *it*, He was greatly displeased and said to them, "Let the little children come to Me, and do not forbid them; for of such is the kingdom of God. Assuredly, I say to you, whoever does not receive the kingdom of God as a little child will by no means enter it." And He took them up in His arms, put *His* hands on them, and blessed them (Mark 10:13–16).

Her children rise up and call her blessed;
Her husband *also*, and he praises her: . . .
(Prov. 31:28).

Relatives

. . . when I call to remembrance the genuine faith that is in you, which dwelt first in your grandmother Lois and your mother Eunice, and I am persuaded is in you also (2 Tim. 1:5).

Behold, how good and how pleasant *it is*
For brethren to dwell together in unity! (Ps. 133:1).

He first found his own brother Simon, and said to him, "We have found the Messiah" (which is translated, the Christ) (John 1:41).

He who says he is in the light, and hates his brother, is in darkness until now. He who loves his brother abides in the light, and there is no cause for stumbling in him (1 John 2:9–10).

Now when Jesus had come into Peter's house, He saw his wife's mother lying sick with a fever. And He touched her hand, and the fever left her. Then she arose and served them (Matt. 8:14–15).

And Naomi said to her two daughters-in-law, "Go, return each to her mother's house. The LORD deal kindly with you, as you have dealt with the dead and with me. The LORD grant that you may find rest, each in the house of her husband." Then she kissed them, and they lifted up their voices and wept (Ruth 1:8–9).

And Jethro, the priest of Midian, Moses' father-in-law, heard of all that God had done for Moses and for Israel His people—that the LORD had brought Israel out of Egypt. . . . So Moses went out to meet his father-in-law, bowed down, and kissed him. And they asked each other about *their* well-being,

and they went into the tent. . . . Then Jethro
rejoiced for all the good which the LORD had done
for Israel, whom He had delivered out of the hand
of the Egyptians (Exod. 18:1,7,9).

Now in Shushan the citadel there was a certain Jew
whose name was Mordecai the son of Jair, the son
of Shimei, the son of Kish, a Benjamite. . . . And
Mordecai had brought up Hadassah, that is, Esther,
his uncle's daughter, for she had neither father nor
mother. The young woman *was* lovely and beautiful.
When her father and mother died, Mordecai took
her as his own daughter (Esther 2:5,7).

Relationships outside the Family

Friends

And the LORD restored Job's losses when he prayed
for his friends. Indeed the LORD gave Job twice as
much as he had before (Job 42:10).

The poor *man* is hated even by his own neighbor,
But the rich *has* many friends (Prov. 14:20).

A friend loves at all times,
And a brother is born for adversity (Prov. 17:17).

A man *who has* friends must himself be friendly,
But there is a friend *who* sticks closer than a brother
  (Prov. 18:24).

Faithful *are* the wounds of a friend,
But the kisses of an enemy *are* deceitful (Prov. 27:6).

Two *are* better than one,
Because they have a good reward for their labor
  (Eccles. 4:9).

"This is My commandment, that you love one
  another as I have loved you. Greater love has no
  one than this, than to lay down one's life for his
  friends. You are My friends if you do whatever I
  command you. No longer do I call you servants,
  for a servant does not know what his master is
  doing; but I have called you friends, for all things
  that I heard from My Father I have made known
  to you" (John 15:12–15).

Neighbors

"You shall not bear false witness against your
neighbor" (Exod. 20:16).

"You shall not covet your neighbor's house; you
shall not covet your neighbor's wife, nor his
manservant, nor his maidservant, nor his ox, nor
his donkey, nor anything that *is* your neighbor's"
(Exod. 20:17).

" 'You shall not take vengeance, nor bear any
grudge against the children of your people, but you
shall love your neighbor as yourself: I *am* the
LORD ' " (Lev. 19:18).

He who is devoid of wisdom despises his neighbor,
But a man of understanding holds his peace
(Prov. 11:12).

Do not forsake your own friend or your father's
  friend,
Nor go to your brother's house in the day of your
  calamity;
For better *is* a neighbor nearby than a brother far
  away (Prov. 27:10).

" 'Let none of you think evil in your heart against
  your neighbor;
And do not love a false oath.
For all these *are* things that I hate,'
Says the LORD" (Zech. 8:17).

"So which of these three do you think was neighbor
to him who fell among the thieves?" And he said,
"He who showed mercy on him." Then Jesus said
to him, "Go and do likewise" (Luke 10:36–37).

Therefore, putting away lying, each one speak truth
with his neighbor, for we are members of one
another (Eph. 4:25).

Elders

Do not rebuke an older man, but exhort *him* as a
father, *the* younger men as brothers, . . .
(1 Tim. 5:1).

Let the elders who rule well be counted worthy of
double honor, especially those who labor in the
word and doctrine (1 Tim. 5:17).

Do not receive an accusation against an elder except
from two or three witnesses (1 Tim. 5:19).

Strangers

"You shall neither mistreat a stranger nor oppress him, for you were strangers in the land of Egypt" (Exod. 22:21).

"Also you shall not oppress a stranger, for you know the heart of a stranger, because you were strangers in the land of Egypt" (Exod. 23:9).

The LORD watches over the strangers;
He relieves the fatherless and widow;
But the way of the wicked He turns upside down
    (Ps. 146:9).

Now, therefore, you are no longer strangers and foreigners, but fellow citizens with the saints and members of the household of God, . . .
(Eph. 2:19).

Enemies

Do not rejoice when your enemy falls,
And do not let your heart be glad when he
    stumbles; . . . (Prov. 24:17).

If your enemy is hungry, give him bread to eat;
And if he is thirsty, give him water to drink; . . .
    (Prov. 25:21).

"You have heard that it was said, 'You shall love your neighbor and hate your enemy.' But I say to you, love your enemies, bless those who curse you, do good to those who hate you, and pray for those who spitefully use you and persecute you, that you may be sons of your Father in heaven; for He makes His sun rise on the evil and on the good, and sends rain on the just and on the unjust" (Matt. 5:43–45).

"Therefore if your enemy hungers, feed him;
If he thirsts, give him a drink;
For in so doing you will heap coals of fire on his head"
  (Rom. 12:20).

Keys to Successful Relationships

Love

Owe no one anything except to love one another, for he who loves another has fulfilled the law. For the commandments, *"You shall not commit adultery," "You shall not murder," "You shall not steal," "You shall not bear false witness," "You shall not covet,"* and if *there is* any other commandment, are *all* summed up in this saying, namely, *"You shall love your neighbor as yourself"* (Rom. 13:8–9).

"Greater love has no one than this, than to lay down one's life for his friends" (John 15:13).

"By this all will know that you are My disciples, if you have love for one another" (John 13:35).

Honesty

"And you shall know the truth, and the truth shall make you free" (John 8:32).

Let not mercy and truth forsake you;
Bind them around your neck.
Write them on the tablet of your heart,

And so find favor and high esteem
In the sight of God and man (Prov. 3:3–4).

"You shall not bear false witness against your
neighbor" (Exod. 20:16).

Righteousness

The fear of the LORD prolongs days,
But the years of the wicked will be shortened.
The hope of the righteous *will be* gladness,
But the expectation of the wicked will perish
   (Prov. 10:27–28).

Righteousness keeps *him whose* way is blameless,
But wickedness overthrows the sinner (Prov. 13:6).

Righteousness exalts a nation,
But sin *is* a reproach to *any* people (Prov. 14:34).

Wisdom

My son, eat honey because *it is* good,
And the honeycomb *which is* sweet to your taste;
So *shall* the knowledge of wisdom *be* to your soul;
If you have found *it*, there is a prospect,
And your hope will not be cut off (Prov. 24:13–14).

Get wisdom! Get understanding!
Do not forget, nor turn away from the words of my
   mouth.
Do not forsake her, and she will preserve you;
Love her, and she will keep you.
Wisdom *is* the principal thing;
Therefore get wisdom.

And in all your getting, get understanding.
Exalt her, and she will promote you;
She will bring you honor, when you embrace her
    (Prov. 4:5–8).

When wisdom enters your heart,
And knowledge is pleasant to your soul,
Discretion will preserve you;
Understanding will keep you, . . . (Prov. 2:10–11).

Faith

"These things I have spoken to you, that in Me you
may have peace. In the world you will have
tribulation; but be of good cheer, I have overcome
the world" (John 16:33).

Now faith is the substance of things hoped for, the
evidence of things not seen. . . . But without faith *it
is* impossible to please *Him*, for he who comes to
God must believe that He is, and *that* He is a
rewarder of those who diligently seek Him
(Heb. 11:1,6).

"And he who reaps receives wages, and gathers
fruit for eternal life, that both he who sows and he
who reaps may rejoice together" (John 4:36).

Trust

Trust in the LORD with all your heart,
And lean not on your own understanding;
In all your ways acknowledge Him,
And He shall direct your paths (Prov. 3:5–6).

The heart of her husband safely trusts her;
So he will have no lack of gain (Prov. 31:11).

"Behold, God *is* my salvation,
I will trust and not be afraid;
'For YAH, the LORD, *is* my strength and *my* song;
He also has become my salvation'" (Isa. 12:2).

Forgiveness

"Take heed to yourselves. If your brother sins
against you, rebuke him; and if he repents, forgive
him. And if he sins against you seven times in a
day, and seven times in a day returns to you,
saying, 'I repent,' you shall forgive him"
(Luke 17:3–4.

Jesus said to him, "If you want to be perfect, go,
sell what you have and give to the poor, and you
will have treasure in heaven; and come, follow
Me." But when the young man heard that saying,
he went away sorrowful, for he had great
possessions (Matt. 18:21–22).

In mercy and truth
Atonement is provided for iniquity;
And by the fear of the LORD *one* departs from evil
(Prov. 16:6).

And forgive us our debts,
As we forgive our debtors (Matt. 6:12).

Now all things *are* of God, who has reconciled us to
Himself through Jesus Christ, and has given us the

ministry of reconciliation, that is, that God was in Christ reconciling the world to Himself, not imputing their trespasses to them, and has committed to us the word of reconciliation. Therefore we are ambassadors for Christ, as though God were pleading through us: we implore *you* on Christ's behalf, be reconciled to God (2 Cor. 5:18–20).

Kindness

Love suffers long *and* is kind; love does not envy; love does not parade itself, is not puffed up; . . . (1 Cor. 13:4).

. . . to godliness brotherly kindness, and to brotherly kindness love (2 Pet. 1:7).

She opens her mouth with wisdom,
And on her tongue *is* the law of kindness (Prov. 31:26).

He has shown you, O man, what *is* good;
And what does the Lord require of you
But to do justly,
To love mercy,
And to walk humbly with your God? (Mic. 6:8).

Peace

Blessed *are* the peacemakers,
For they shall be called sons of God (Matt. 5:9).

Better *is* a little with the fear of the Lord,
Than great treasure with trouble (Prov. 15:16).

The work of righteousness will be peace,
And the effect of righteousness, quietness and
    assurance forever (Isa. 32:17).

For thus says the LORD:

"Behold, I will extend peace to her like a river,
And the glory of the Gentiles like a flowing stream.
Then you shall feed;
On *her* sides shall you be carried,
And be dandled on *her* knees" (Isa. 66:12).

. . . and to esteem them very highly in love for
their work's sake. Be at peace among yourselves
(1 Thess. 5:13).

If it is possible, as much as depends on you, live
peaceably with all men (Rom. 12:18).

Joy

A man has joy by the answer of his mouth,
And a word *spoken* in due season, how good *it is!*
    (Prov. 15:23).

The light of the eyes rejoices the heart,
And a good report makes the bones healthy
    (Prov. 15:30).

My son, if your heart is wise,
My heart will rejoice—indeed, I myself;
Yes, my inmost being will rejoice
When your lips speak right things (Prov. 23:15–16).

= 13 =

Communication

Communication is one of the unique characteristics of human beings. It reflects the image of God in which we were created. However, our ability to communicate may be used both positively or negatively. That is why the apostle James wrote: "Out of the same mouth proceed blessing and cursing. My brethren, these things ought not to be so" (James 3:10).

Learning to communicate effectively is vital for family living. It is the key to corporate understanding and personal growth. Families that communicate well develop strong unity and loyalty. They understand and appreciate one another because they can express their personal concerns lovingly and openly.

Effective communication depends upon honesty, sincerity, love and wisdom. It often expresses itself in counsel, encouragement and forgiveness. Communication is the key to marital happiness and parental guidance. It has the potential of binding the hearts and lives of every family member together in unity.

Communication is something we learn by doing. The more we do it, the better we become at it. Don't hide all your feelings within yourself. Learn to express your feelings and communicate with each other in love and kindness. Be positive and encouraging and you will be a blessing to one another.

Speak the Truth in Love

Honesty Is the Best Policy

. . . but, speaking the truth in love, may grow up in all things into Him who is the head—Christ— (Eph. 4:15).

Therefore, putting away lying, each one speak truth with his neighbor, for we are members of one another (Eph. 4:25).

"Now therefore, fear the LORD, serve Him in sincerity and in truth, and put away the gods which your fathers served on the other side of the River and in Egypt. Serve the LORD!" (Josh. 24:14).

He who walks uprightly,
And works righteousness,
And speaks the truth in his heart; . . . (Ps. 15:2).

Behold, You desire truth in the inward parts,
And in the hidden *part* You will make me to know
    wisdom (Ps. 51:6).

Mercy and truth have met together;
Righteousness and peace have kissed *each other*
    (Ps. 85:10).

162

And take not the word of truth utterly out of my
    mouth,
For I have hoped in Your ordinances (Ps. 119:43).

These *are* the things you shall do:
Speak each man the truth to his neighbor;
Give judgment in your gate for truth, justice, and
    peace; . . . (Zech. 8:16).

The law of truth was in his mouth,
And injustice was not found on his lips.
He walked with Me in peace and equity,
And turned many away from iniquity (Mal. 2:6).

"But let your 'Yes' be 'Yes,' and your 'No,' 'No.' For
whatever is more than these is from the evil one"
(Matt. 5:37).

Guard Your Tongue
I said, "I will guard my ways,
Lest I sin with my tongue;
I will restrain my mouth with a muzzle,
While the wicked are before me" (Ps. 39:1).

An evildoer gives heed to false lips;
A liar listens eagerly to a spiteful tongue
    (Prov. 17:4).

He who has a deceitful heart finds no good,
And he who has a perverse tongue falls into evil
    (Prov. 17:20).

He who hates, disguises *it* with his lips,
And lays up deceit within himself;

When he speaks kindly, do not believe him,
For *there are* seven abominations in his heart;
Though his hatred is covered by deceit,
His wickedness will be revealed before the *whole*
   congregation (Prov. 26:24–26).

A lying tongue hates *those who are* crushed by it,
And a flattering mouth works ruin (Prov. 26:28).

The tongue of the wise uses knowledge rightly,
But the mouth of fools pours forth foolishness. . . .
A wholesome tongue *is* a tree of life,
But perverseness in it breaks the spirit (Prov.
   15:2, 4).

A man has joy by the answer of his mouth,
And a word *spoken* in due season, how good *it is!*
   (Prov. 15:23).

The thoughts of the wicked *are* an abomination to
   the LORD,
But *the words* of the pure *are* pleasant (Prov. 15:26).

She opens her mouth with wisdom,
And on her tongue *is* the law of kindness
   (Prov. 31:26).

Let your speech always *be* with grace, seasoned with
salt, that you may know how you ought to answer
each one (Col. 4:6).

And the tongue *is* a fire, a world of iniquity. The
tongue is so set among our members that it defiles
the whole body, and sets on fire the course of

nature; and it is set on fire by hell. . . . But no man can tame the tongue. *It is* an unruly evil, full of deadly poison (James 3:6,8).

"Brood of vipers! How can you, being evil, speak good things? For out of the abundance of the heart the mouth speaks" (Matt. 12:34).

Say the Truth with Love

He who covers a transgression seeks love,
But he who repeats a matter separates *the best of*
    friends (Prov. 17:9).

The north wind brings forth rain,
And a backbiting tongue an angry countenance
    (Prov. 25:23).

The mouth of the righteous brings forth wisdom,
But the perverse tongue will be cut out.
The lips of the righteous know what is acceptable,
But the mouth of the wicked *what is* perverse
    (Prov. 10:31–32).

The tongue of the wise uses knowledge rightly,
But the mouth of fools pours forth foolishness
    (Prov. 15:2).

The heart of the righteous studies how to answer,
But the mouth of the wicked pours forth evil
    (Prov. 15:28).

Hatred stirs up strife,
But love covers all sins (Prov. 10:12).

Open rebuke *is* better
Than love carefully concealed (Prov. 27:5).

He who loves purity of heart
And has grace on his lips,
The king *will be* his friend (Prov. 22:11).

Express Mercy and Forgiveness

Mercy Brings Blessing and Honor

Let not mercy and truth forsake you;
Bind them around your neck,
Write them on the tablet of your heart,
And so find favor and high esteem
In the sight of God and man (Prov. 3:3–4).

The merciful man does good for his own soul,
But *he who is* cruel troubles his own flesh
(Prov. 11:17).

He who despises his neighbor sins;
But he who has mercy on the poor, happy *is* he.
Do they not go astray who devise evil?
But mercy and truth *belong to* those who devise
good (Prov. 14:21–22).

He who oppresses the poor reproaches his Maker,
But he who honors Him has mercy on the needy
(Prov. 14:31).

He who follows righteousness and mercy
Finds life, righteousness and honor (Prov. 21:21).

Mercy and truth preserve the king,
And by lovingkindness he upholds his throne
(Prov. 20:28).

Surely goodness and mercy shall follow me
All the days of my life;
And I will dwell in the house of the LORD
Forever (Ps. 23:6).

Remember, O LORD, Your tender mercies and Your
lovingkindness,
For they *have been* from of old (Ps. 25:6).

Who redeems your life from destruction,
Who crowns you with lovingkindness and tender
mercies, . . . (Ps. 103:4).

"Blessed *are* the merciful, for they shall obtain
mercy" (Matt. 5:7).

Forgiveness Restores
Hatred stirs up strife,
But love covers all sins (Prov. 10:12).

The discretion of a man makes him slow to anger,
And *it is to* his glory to overlook a transgression
(Prov. 19:11).

In mercy and truth
Atonement is provided for iniquity;
And by the fear of the LORD *one* departs from evil
(Prov. 16:6).

He who covers his sins will not prosper,
But whoever confesses and forsakes *them* will have
mercy (Prov. 28:13).

He who covers a transgression seeks love,
But he who repeats a matter separates *the best of*
friends (Prov. 17:9).

"And whenever you stand praying, if you have
anything against anyone, forgive him, that your
Father in heaven may also forgive you your
trespasses" (Mark 11:25).

Then Peter came to Him and said, "Lord, how
often shall my brother sin against me, and I forgive
him? Up to seven times?" Jesus said to him, "I do
not say to you, up to seven times, but up to
seventy times seven" (Matt. 18:21,22).

"Take heed to yourselves. If your brother sins
against you, rebuke him; and if he repents, forgive
him" (Luke 17:3).

Brethren, if a man is overtaken in any trespass, you
who *are* spiritual restore such a one in a spirit of
gentleness, considering yourself lest you also be
tempted (Gal. 6:1).

Give Wisdom and Guidance

Seek the Lord
Trust in the Lord with all your heart,
And lean not on your own understanding;

Communication

In all your ways acknowledge Him,
And He shall direct your paths (Prov. 3:5–6).

The preparations of the heart *belong* to man,
But the answer of the tongue *is* from the LORD
   (Prov. 16:1).

Commit your works to the LORD,
And your thoughts will be established (Prov. 16:3).

Listen to Your Parents

Listen to your father who begot you,
And do not despise your mother when she is
   old. . . .
My son, give me your heart,
And let your eyes observe my ways
   (Prov. 23:22,26).

A wise son *heeds* his father's instruction,
But a scoffer does not listen to rebuke (Prov. 13:1).

Hear, *my* children, the instruction of a father,
And give attention to know understanding;
For I give you good doctrine:
Do not forsake my law.
When I was my father's son,
Tender and the only one in the sight of my mother,
He also taught me, and said to me:
"Let your heart retain my words;
Keep my commands, and live" (Prov. 4:1–4).

My son, do not forget my law,
But let your heart keep my commands;

For length of days and long life
And peace they will add to you (Prov. 3:1–2).

My son, hear the instruction of your father,
And do not forsake the law of your mother;
For they *will be* graceful ornaments on your head,
And chains about your neck (Prov. 1:8–9).

Therefore hear me now, *my* children,
And do not depart from the words of my mouth
(Prov. 5:7).

My son, keep my words,
And treasure my commands within you.
Keep my commands and live,
And my law as the apple of your eye.
Bind them on your fingers;
Write them on the tablet of your heart (Prov. 7:1–3).

Accept Wise Counsel
Your testimonies also *are* my delight
And my counselors (Ps. 119:24).

"To you, O men, I call,
And my voice *is* to the sons of men" (Prov. 8:4).

Give *instruction* to a wise *man*, and he will be still
wiser;
Teach a just *man*, and he will increase in learning
(Prov. 9:9).

Where *there is* no counsel, the people fall;
But in the multitude of counselors *there is* safety
(Prov. 11:14).

The way of a fool *is* right in his own eyes,
But he who heeds counsel *is* wise (Prov. 12:15).

Without counsel, plans go awry,
But in the multitude of counselors they are
    established (Prov. 15:22).

Listen to counsel and receive instruction,
That you may be wise in your latter days
    (Prov. 19:20).

Blessed *is* the man
Who walks not in the counsel of the ungodly,
Nor stands in the path of sinners,
Nor sits in the seat of the scornful; . . .
    (Ps. 1:1).

The counsel of the LORD stands forever,
The plans of His heart to all generations (Ps. 33:11).

Give Hope and Encouragement

Avoid Harmful Gossip

A talebearer reveals secrets,
But he who is of a faithful spirit conceals a matter
    (Prov. 11:13).

An ungodly man digs up evil,
And *it is* on his lips like a burning fire.
A perverse man sows strife,
And a whisperer separates the best of friends
    (Prov. 16:27–28).

Where *there is* no wood, the fire goes out;
And where *there is* no talebearer, strife ceases
(Prov. 26:20).

Do not curse the king, even in your thought;
Do not curse the rich, even in your bedroom;
For a bird of the air may carry your voice,
And a bird in flight may tell the matter
(Eccles. 10:20).

For I fear lest, when I come, I shall not find you
such as I wish, and *that* I shall be found by you
such as you do not wish; lest *there be* contentions,
jealousies, outbursts of wrath, selfish ambitions,
backbitings, whisperings, conceits, tumults; . . .
(2 Cor. 12:20).

But reject profane and old wives' fables, and
exercise yourself *rather* to godliness (1 Tim. 4:7).

All the words of my mouth *are* with righteousness;
Nothing crooked or perverse *is* in them (Prov. 18:8).

Express Positive Hope
Therefore my heart is glad, and my glory rejoices;
My flesh also will rest in hope (Ps. 16:9).

Hope deferred makes the heart sick,
But *when* the desire comes, *it is* a tree of life
(Prov. 13:12).

And not only *that*, but we also glory in tribulations,
knowing that tribulation produces perseverance;
and perseverance, character; and character, hope.

Now hope does not disappoint, because the love of God has been poured out in our hearts by the Holy Spirit who was given to us (Rom. 5:3–5).

Rejoicing in hope, patient in tribulation, continuing steadfastly in prayer; . . . (Rom. 12:12).

Now may the God of hope fill you with all joy and peace in believing, that you may abound in hope by the power of the Holy Spirit (Rom. 15:13).

. . . the eyes of your understanding being enlightened; that you may know what is the hope of His calling, what are the riches of the glory of His inheritance in the saints, and what *is* the exceeding greatness of His power toward us who believe, according to the working of His mighty power . . . (Eph. 1:18–19).

Thus God, determining to show more abundantly to the heirs of promise the immutability of His counsel, confirmed *it* by an oath, that by two immutable things, in which *it is* impossible for God to lie, we might have strong consolation, who have fled for refuge to lay hold of the hope set before *us*. This *hope* we have as an anchor of the soul, both sure and steadfast, and which enters the Presence *behind* the veil, . . . (Heb. 6:17–19).

Now faith is the substance of things hoped for, the evidence of things not seen (Heb. 11:1).

And everyone who has this hope in Him purifies himself, just as He is pure (1 John 3:3).

Give Practical Encouragement

"Only be strong and very courageous, that you may observe to do according to all the law which Moses My servant commanded you; do not turn from it to the right hand or to the left, that you may prosper wherever you go" (Josh. 1:7).

Then David was greatly distressed, for the people spoke of stoning him, because the soul of all the people was grieved, every man for his sons and his daughters. But David strengthened himself in the LORD his God (1 Sam. 30:6).

" 'Fear not, for I *am* with you;
Be not dismayed, for I *am* your God.
I will strengthen you,
Yes, I will help you,
I will uphold you with My righteous right hand' "
    (Isa. 41:10).

But now, thus says the LORD, who created you, O
    Jacob,
And He who formed you, O Israel:
"Fear not, for I have redeemed you;
I have called *you* by your name;
You *are* Mine" (Isa. 43:1).

"The Lord God has given Me
The tongue of the learned,
That I should know how to speak
A word in season to *him who is* weary.
He awakens Me morning by morning,

He awakens My ear
To hear as the learned" (Isa. 50:4).

But immediately Jesus spoke to them, saying, "Be of good cheer! It is I; do not be afraid" (Matt. 14:27).

. . . strengthening the souls of the disciples, exhorting *them* to continue in the faith, and *saying*, "We must through many tribulations enter the kingdom of God" (Acts 14:22).

"And now I urge you to take heart, for there will be no loss of life among you, but only of the ship" (Acts 27:22).

Now we exhort you, brethren, warn those who are unruly, comfort the fainthearted, uphold the weak, be patient with all (1 Thess. 5:14).

. . . but exhort one another daily, while it is called *"Today,"* lest any of you be hardened through the deceitfulness of sin (Heb. 3:13).

. . . not forsaking the assembling of ourselves together, as *is* the manner of some, but exhorting *one another*, and so much the more as you see the Day approaching (Heb. 10:25).

═14═

Problems and Trials

Life is filled with problems. The longer we live the more problems we must solve. They challenge our faith and stretch our patience. Each new difficulty provides new options for personal growth and maturity.

The Bible reminds us: "Yes, and all who desire to live godly in Christ Jesus will suffer persecution" (2 Tim. 3:12). Some of our problems are caused by ourselves, while some are brought on by others. Either way, we must learn how to face each one honestly and then appropriate the all-sufficient grace of God to meet our needs.

One of the purposes of trials and difficulties is to teach us patience (see James 1:2–3). It is in these times that our faith grows and our walk with God matures. No matter what difficulties you may be experiencing, never lose sight of the fact that God is at work in your life.

In every problem of life, God's purposes are greater than our frustrations. His plans are more wonderful than our hopes. His grace is greater than our difficulties. And His love is sufficient to sustain us in every trial. Trust Him; He will not let you down!

Suffering Is a Part of Life

Christ Suffered for Us

For to this you were called, because Christ also suffered for us, leaving us an example, that you should follow His steps: . . . (1 Pet. 2:21).

For Christ also suffered once for sins, the just for the unjust, that He might bring us to God, being put to death in the flesh but made alive by the Spirit, . . . (1 Pet. 3:18).

Therefore, since Christ suffered for us in the flesh, arm yourselves also with the same mind, for he who has suffered in the flesh has ceased from sin, . . . (1 Pet. 4:1).

"The Son of Man must suffer many things, and be rejected by the elders and chief priests and scribes, and be killed, and be raised the third day" (Luke 9:22).

"Ought not the Christ to have suffered these things and to enter into His glory?" (Luke 24:26).

For in that He Himself has suffered, being tempted, He is able to aid those who are tempted (Heb. 2:18).

Seeing then that we have a great High Priest who has passed through the heavens, Jesus the Son of God, let us hold fast *our* confession. For we do not

177

have a High Priest who cannot sympathize with our weaknesses, but was in all *points* tempted as *we are, yet* without sin. Let us therefore come boldly to the throne of grace, that we may obtain mercy and find grace to help in time of need (Heb. 4:15–16).

We Share in His Suffering

. . . that I may know Him and the power of His resurrection, and the fellowship of His sufferings, being conformed to His death, . . . (Phil. 3:10).

. . . but rejoice to the extent that you partake of Christ's sufferings, that when His glory is revealed, you may also be glad with exceeding joy (1 Pet. 4:13).

. . . though He was a Son, *yet* He learned obedience by the things which He suffered. And having been perfected, He became the author of eternal salvation to all who obey Him, . . (Heb. 5:8–9).

If we endure,
　We shall also reign with *Him*.
If we deny *Him*,
　He also will deny us (2 Tim. 2:12).

. . . and if children, then heirs—heirs of God and joint heirs with Christ, if indeed we suffer with *Him*, that we may also be glorified together (Rom. 8:17).

But indeed I also count all things loss for the excellence of the knowledge of Christ Jesus my

Lord, for whom I have suffered the loss of all things, and count them as rubbish, that I may gain Christ . . . (Phil. 3:8).

And our hope for you *is* steadfast, because we know that as you are partakers of the sufferings, so also *you will partake* of the consolation (2 Cor. 1:7).

Suffering Produces Positive Results

Patience

My brethren, count it all joy when you fall into various trials, knowing that the testing of your faith produces patience. But let patience have *its* perfect work, that you may be perfect and complete, lacking nothing (James 1:2–4).

Humility

Therefore strengthen the hands which hang down, and the feeble knees, and make straight paths for your feet, so that what is lame may not be *dislocated*, but rather be healed (Heb. 13:12–13).

Obedience

. . . though He was a Son, *yet* He learned obedience by the things which He suffered (Heb. 5:8).

Joy

Moreover, brethren, we make known to you the grace of God bestowed on the churches of Macedonia: that in a great trial of affliction the

abundance of their joy and their deep poverty
abounded in the riches of their liberality
(2 Cor. 8:1–2).

. . . but rejoice to the extent that you partake of
Christ's sufferings, that when His glory is revealed,
you may also be glad with exceeding joy
(1 Pet. 4:13).

Boldness

But even after we had suffered before and were
spitefully treated at Philippi, as you know, we were
bold in our God to speak to you the gospel of God
in much conflict (1 Thess. 2:2).

Purpose

Have you suffered so many things in vain—if
indeed *it was* in vain? (Gal. 3:4).

Comfort

Blessed *be* the God and Father of our Lord Jesus
Christ, the Father of mercies and God of all
comfort, who comforts us in all our tribulation, that
we may be able to comfort those who are in any
trouble, with the comfort with which we ourselves
are comforted by God. For as the sufferings of
Christ abound in us, so our consolation also
abounds through Christ. Now if we are afflicted, *it is*
for your consolation and salvation, which is
effective for enduring the same sufferings which we
also suffer. Or if we are comforted, *it is* for your
consolation and salvation. And our hope for you *is*

steadfast, because we know that as you are partakers of the sufferings, so also *you will partake* of the consolation (2 Cor. 1:3–7).

Suffering Is Temporary

Limited to the Present

For I consider that the sufferings of this present time are not worthy *to be compared* with the glory which shall be revealed in us (Rom. 8:18).

Therefore we do not lose heart. Even though our outward man is perishing, yet the inward *man* is being renewed day by day. For our light affliction, which is but for a moment, is working for us a far more exceeding *and* eternal weight of glory, while we do not look at the things which are seen, but at the things which are not seen. For the things which are seen *are* temporary, but the things which are not seen *are* eternal (2 Cor. 4:16–18).

In this you greatly rejoice, though now for a little while, if need be, you have been grieved by various trials, that the genuineness of your faith, *being* much more precious than gold that perishes, though it is tested by fire, may be found to praise, honor, and glory at the revelation of Jesus Christ, . . . (1 Pet. 1:6–7).

Enables Us to Endure the Present

And we labor, working with our own hands. Being reviled, we bless; being persecuted, we endure *it;* . . . (1 Cor. 4:12).

If we endure,
We shall also reign with *Him.*
If we deny *Him,* He also will deny us (2 Tim. 2:12).

My brethren, take the prophets, who spoke in the name of the Lord, as an example of suffering and patience. Indeed we count them blessed who endure. You have heard of the perseverance of Job and seen the end *intended by* the Lord—that the Lord is very compassionate and merciful (James 5:10–11).

Fades in Light of Future Glory

The elders who are among you I exhort, I who am a fellow elder and a witness of the sufferings of Christ, and also a partaker of the glory that will be revealed: . . . (1 Pet. 5:1).

But may the God of all grace, who called us to His eternal glory by Christ Jesus, after you have suffered a while, perfect, establish, strengthen, and settle *you.* To Him *be* the glory and the dominion forever and ever. Amen (1 Pet. 5:10–11).

For I consider that the sufferings of this present time are not worthy *to be compared* with the glory which shall be revealed in us (Rom. 8:18).

How to Handle Suffering

Deny Yourself

Then Jesus said to His disciples, "If anyone desires to come after Me, let him deny himself, and take up his cross, and follow Me" (Matt. 16:24).

But Jesus answered and said, "You do not know what you ask. Are you able to drink the cup that I am about to drink, and be baptized with the baptism that I am baptized with?" They said to Him, "We are able" (Matt. 20:22).

Accept the Process

"For I will show him how many things he must suffer for My name's sake" (Acts 9:16).

For to you, it has been granted on behalf of Christ, not only to believe in Him, but also to suffer for His sake, . . . (Phil. 1:29).

But even if you should suffer for righteousness' sake, *you are* blessed. *"And do not be afraid of their threats, nor be troubled"* (1 Pet. 3:14).

By faith Moses, when he became of age, refused to be called the son of Pharaoh's daughter, choosing rather to suffer affliction with the people of God than to enjoy the passing pleasures of sin, esteeming the reproach of Christ greater riches than the treasures in Egypt; for he looked to the reward. By faith he forsook Egypt, not fearing the wrath of the king; for he endured as seeing Him who is invisible (Heb. 11:24–27).

Pray

Is anyone among you suffering? Let him pray. Is anyone cheerful? Let him sing psalms (James 5:13).

For to this you were called, because Christ also suffered for us, leaving us an example, that you should follow His steps:

> "Who committed no sin,
> Nor was guile found in His mouth";

who, when He was reviled, did not revile in return; when He suffered, He did not threaten, but committed *Himself* to Him who judges righteously . . . (1 Pet. 2:21–23).

Fear Not

"Do not fear any of those things which you are about to suffer. Indeed, the devil is about to throw *some* of you into prison, that you may be tested, and you will have tribulation ten days. Be faithful until death, and I will give you the crown of life" (Rev. 2:10).

Follow Christ's Example

For what credit *is it* if, when you are beaten for your faults, you take it patiently? But when you do good and suffer *for it*, if you take it patiently, this is commendable before God (1 Pet. 2:20).

For *it is* better, if it is the will of God, to suffer for doing good than for doing evil (1 Pet. 3:17).

Yet if *anyone suffers* as a Christian, let him not be ashamed, but let him glorify God in this matter (1 Pet. 4:16).

Commit Your Problems to God

For this *is* commendable, if because of conscience toward God one endures grief, suffering wrongfully. For what credit *is it* if, when you are beaten for your faults, you take it patiently? But when you do good and suffer *for it,* if you take it patiently, this *is* commendable before God. For to this you were called, because Christ also suffered for us, leaving us an example, that you should follow His steps:

> "Who committed no sin,
> Nor was guile found in His mouth";

who, when He was reviled, did not revile in return; when He suffered, He did not threaten, but committed *Himself* to Him who judges righteously; who Himself bore our sins in His own body on the tree, that we, having died to sins, might live for righteousness—by whose stripes you were healed (1 Pet. 2:19–24).

Accept His Sufficient Grace

And God *is* able to make all grace abound toward you, that you, always having all sufficiency in all *things,* have an abundance for every good work (2 Cor. 9:8).

And lest I should be exalted above measure by the abundance of the revelations, a thorn in the flesh was given to me, a messenger of Satan to buffet

185

me, lest I be exalted above measure. Concerning this thing I pleaded with the Lord three times that it might depart from me. And He said to me, "My grace is sufficient for you, for My strength is made perfect in weakness." Therefore most gladly I will rather boast in my infirmities, that the power of Christ may rest upon me. Therefore I take pleasure in infirmities, in reproaches, in needs, in persecutions, in distresses, for Christ's sake. For when I am weak, then I am strong (2 Cor. 12:7–10).

Share Your Burdens with Others

And if one member suffers, all the members suffer with *it;* or if one member is honored, all the members rejoice with *it* (1 Cor. 12:26).

Bear one another's burdens, and so fulfill the law of Christ (Gal. 6:2).

Yes, and all who desire to live godly in Christ Jesus will suffer persecution (2 Tim. 3:12).

$=15=$

Finances

The laws of economics and principles of financial prosperity are clearly outlined in the Bible. The Scriptures speak often about buying and selling, the legitimacy of free market enterprise and the right of property ownership. Wealth itself is seen as God's blessing (see Prov. 10:22).

The Bible also reminds us, however, that money alone cannot buy happiness. Wealth itself is only temporary. It cannot produce spiritual reality, for it is temporal in nature. Our attitude toward money and possessions reflects our values. When we value things more than God, we can never know His real blessing upon our lives.

Learning to handle money properly was often the subject of Jesus' parables (see Matthew 25 and Luke 16). Stewardship is clearly taught in Scripture. It is the concept of responsible money management. Good stewardship is essential in both one's family life and business life. We are all responsible for what we do with the things God gives us in life. Money is a necessary part of life. Learn to earn it, save it and budget it to meet your family's needs. Our money should be managed wisely, invested carefully, spent cautiously and given joyfully.

Ultimately, money is to be used to God's glory. When we invest our money to promote the gospel of Jesus Christ, we are investing in God's work. Every family seeking His financial blessing needs to develop the "grace of giving." Our investment in the lives of others teaches our children the importance of giving. It shows by example that we are not greedy with our possessions, but considerate of others. It also reveals that God is first in our lives.

God Is the Giver of Wealth and Prosperity

God Gives Us the Ability to Earn

"And you shall remember the LORD your God, for *it is* He who gives you power to get wealth, that He may establish His covenant which He swore to your fathers, as *it is* this day" (Deut. 8:18).

As for every man to whom God has given riches and wealth, and given him power to eat of it, to receive his heritage and rejoice in his labor—this *is* the gift of God (Eccles. 5:19).

A man to whom God has given riches and wealth and honor, so that he lacks nothing for himself of all he desires; yet God does not give him power to eat of it, but a foreigner consumes it. This *is* vanity, and it *is* an evil affliction (Eccles. 6:2).

God Gives Us Dominion Over the Earth

Then God blessed them, and God said to them, "Be fruitful and multiply; fill the earth and subdue it; have dominion over the fish of the sea, over the birds of the air, and over every living thing that moves on the earth" (Gen. 1:28).

You have made him to have dominion over the
  works of Your hands;
You have put all *things* under his feet, . . . (Ps. 8:6).

As it is written, *"He who gathered much had nothing left over, and he who gathered little had no lack"* (2 Cor. 8:15).

God Expects Responsible Stewardship

"He who *is* faithful in *what is* least is faithful also in much; and he who is unjust in *what is* least is unjust also in much. Therefore if you have not been faithful in the unrighteous mammon, who will commit to your trust the true *riches*?" (Luke 16:10–11).

"For *the kingdom of heaven is* like a man traveling to a far country, *who* called his own servants and delivered his goods to them. And to one he gave five talents, to another two, and to another one, to each according to his own ability; and immediately

189

he went on a journey. Then he who had received the five talents went and traded with them, and made another five talents. And likewise he who *had received* two gained two more also. But he who had received one went and dug in the ground, and hid his lord's money. After a long time the lord of those servants came and settled accounts with them. So he who had received five talents came and brought five other talents, saying, 'Lord, you delivered to me five talents; look, I have gained five more talents besides them.' His lord said to him, 'Well *done*, good and faithful servant; you were faithful over a few things, I will make you ruler over many things. Enter into the joy of your lord.' He also who had received two talents came and said, 'Lord, you delivered to me two talents; look, I have gained two more talents besides them.' His lord said to him, 'Well *done*, good and faithful servant; you have been faithful over a few things, I will make you ruler over many things. Enter into the joy of your lord.' Then he who had received the one talent came and said, 'Lord, I knew you to be a hard man, reaping where you have not sown, and gathering where you have not scattered seed. And I was afraid, and went and hid your talent in the ground. Look, *there* you have *what is* yours.' But his lord answered and said to him, 'You wicked and lazy servant, you knew that I reap where I have not sown, and gather where I have not scattered seed. Therefore you ought to have deposited my money with the bankers, and at my coming I would have received back my own with interest. Therefore take the talent from him, and give *it* to him who has ten talents. For to everyone who has, more will be given, and he will have abundance; but from him who does not have, even what he has will be taken away. And cast the unprofitable servant into the outer darkness. There will be weeping and gnashing of teeth'" (Matt. 25:14–30).

God Blesses Diligence and Hard Work

He who deals *with* a slack hand becomes poor,
But the hand of the diligent makes *one* rich
(Prov. 10:4).

The blessing of the LORD makes *one* rich,
And He adds no sorrow with it (Prov. 10:22).

And let the beauty of the LORD our God be upon us,
And establish the work of our hands for us;
Yes, establish the work of our hands (Ps. 90:17).

When you eat the labor of your hands,
You *shall be* happy, and *it shall be* well with you
(Ps. 128:2).

The soul of a sluggard desires, and *has* nothing;
But the soul of the diligent shall be made rich
(Prov. 13:4).

God Condemns Laziness and Slothfulness

Go to the ant, you sluggard!
Consider her ways and be wise,

Which, having no captain,
Overseer or ruler,
Provides her supplies in the summer,
And gathers her food in the harvest.
How long will you slumber, O sluggard?
When will you rise from your sleep?
A little sleep, a little slumber,
A little folding of the hands to sleep—
So shall your poverty come on you like a robber,
And your need like an armed man (Prov. 6:6–11).

Slothfulness casts *one* into a deep sleep,
And an idle person will suffer hunger (Prov. 19:15).

The sluggard will not plow because of winter;
Therefore he will beg during the harvest.
And *have* nothing (Prov. 20:4).

The slothful *man* says, "*There is* a lion outside!
I shall be slain in the streets!" (Prov. 22:13).

As a door turns on its hinges,
So *does* the slothful *turn* on his bed (Prov. 26:14).

And besides they learn *to be* idle, wandering about
from house to house, and not only idle but also
gossips and busybodies, saying things which they
ought not (1 Tim. 5:13).

God Recognizes the Value of Wealth in this World

The rich man's wealth *is* his strong city,
And like a high wall in his own esteem
   (Prov. 18:11).

"And I say to you, make friends for yourselves by unrighteous mammon, that when you fail, they may receive you into everlasting habitations"
(Luke 16:9).

He Warns That Wealth Is Temporary

Wealth *gained by* dishonesty will be diminished,
But he who gathers by labor will increase
(Prov. 13:11).

Will you set your eyes on that which is not?
For *riches* certainly make themselves wings;
They fly away like an eagle *toward* heaven
(Prov. 23:5).

Then I hated all my labor in which I had toiled under the sun, because I must leave it to the man who will come after me. And who knows whether he will be a wise *man* or a fool? Yet he will rule over all my labor in which I toiled and in which I have shown myself wise under the sun. This also *is* vanity. Therefore I turned my heart and despaired of all the labor in which I had toiled under the sun. For there is a man whose labor *is* with wisdom, knowledge, and skill; yet he must leave his heritage to a man who has not labored for it. This also *is* vanity and a great evil (Eccles. 2:18–21).

For we brought nothing into *this* world, *and it is* certain we can carry nothing out (1 Tim. 6:7).

For no sooner has the sun risen with a burning heat than it withers the grass; its flower falls, and its beautiful appearance perishes. So the rich man also will fade away in his pursuits (James 1:11).

Money Alone Cannot Bring Happiness

Seek God First

"Do not lay up for yourselves, treasures on earth where moth and rust destroy and where thieves break in and steal; but lay up for yourselves treasures in heaven, where neither moth nor rust destroys and where thieves do not break in and steal. For where your treasure is, there your heart will be also" (Matt. 6:19–21).

"No one can serve two masters; for either he will hate the one and love the other, or else he will be loyal to the one and despise the other. You cannot serve God and mammon. Therefore I say to you, do not worry about your life, what you will eat or what you will drink; nor about your body, what you will put on. Is not life more than food and the body more than clothing? Look at the birds of the air, for they neither sow nor reap nor gather into barns; yet your heavenly Father feeds them. Are you not of more value than they? Which of you by worrying can add one cubit to his stature? So why do you worry about clothing? Consider the lilies of the field, how they grow: they neither toil nor spin; and yet I say to you that even Solomon in all his glory was not arrayed like one of these. Now if God so clothes the grass of the field, which today is, and tomorrow is thrown into the oven, *will He* not much more *clothe* you, O you of little faith? Therefore do not worry, saying, 'What shall we eat?' or 'What shall we drink?' or 'What shall we wear?' For after all these things the Gentiles seek. For your heavenly Father knows that you need all these things. But seek first the kingdom of God and His righteousness, and all these things shall be added to you" (Matt. 6:24–33).

A *good* name is to be chosen rather than great riches,
Loving favor rather than silver and gold (Prov. 22:1).

Do not overwork to be rich;
Because of your own understanding, cease!
(Prov. 23:4).

Then Peter said, "Silver and gold I do not have, but what I do have I give you: In the name of Jesus Christ of Nazareth, rise up and walk" (Acts 3:6).

Beware of the Dangers of Materialism

"No servant can serve two masters; for either he will hate the one and love the other, or else he will be loyal to the one and despise the other. You cannot serve God and mammon" (Luke 16:13).

For the love of money is a root of all *kinds of* evil, for which some have strayed from the faith in their greediness, and pierced themselves through with many sorrows (1 Tim. 6:10).

A faithful man will abound with blessings,
But he who hastens to be rich will not go
  unpunished (Prov. 28:20).

He who loves silver will not be satisfied with silver;
Nor he who loves abundance, with increase.
This also *is* vanity (Eccles. 5:10).

The sleep of a laboring man *is* sweet,
Whether he eats little or much;
But the abundance of the rich will not permit him
  to sleep (Eccles. 5:12).

Wealth Cannot Save
And the disciples were astonished at His words.
But Jesus answered again and said to them,
"Children, how hard it is for those who trust in
riches to enter the kingdom of God!" (Mark 10:24).

"But woe to you who are rich,
For you have received your consolation" (Luke
  6:24).

And He said to them, "Take heed and beware of
covetousness, for one's life does not consist in the
abundance of the things he possesses." Then He
spoke a parable to them, saying: "The ground of a
certain rich man yielded plentifully. And he
thought within himself, saying, 'What shall I do,
since I have no room to store my crops?' So he
said, 'I will do this: I will pull down my barns and
build greater, and there I will store all my crops and
my goods. And I will say to my soul, "Soul, you

have many goods laid up for many years; take your ease; eat, drink, *and* be merry."' But God said to him, *'You* fool! This night your soul will be required of you; then whose will those things be which you have provided?' So *is* he who lays up treasure for himself, and is not rich toward God" (Luke 12:15–21).

Jesus said to him, "If you want to be perfect, go, sell what you have and give to the poor, and you will have treasure in heaven; and come, follow Me." But when the young man heard that saying, he went away sorrowful, for he had great possessions. Then Jesus said to His disciples, "Assuredly, I say to you that it is hard for a rich man to enter the kingdom of heaven. And again I say to you, it is easier for a camel to go through the eye of a needle than for a rich man to enter the kingdom of God" (Matt. 19:21–24).

"There was a certain rich man who was clothed in purple and fine linen and fared sumptuously every day. But there was a certain beggar named Lazarus, full of sores, who was laid at his gate, desiring to be fed with the crumbs which fell from the rich man's table. Moreover the dogs came and licked his sores. So it was that the beggar died, and was carried by the angels to Abraham's bosom. The rich man also died and was buried. And being in torments in Hades, he lifted up his eyes and saw Abraham afar off, and Lazarus in his bosom. Then he cried and said, 'Father Abraham, have mercy on me, and

send Lazarus that he may dip the tip of his finger in water and cool my tongue; for I am tormented in this flame.' But Abraham said, 'Son, remember that in your lifetime you received your good things, and likewise Lazarus evil things; but now he is comforted and you are tormented'"
(Luke 16:19–25).

Wealth Cannot Be Kept

For he sees *that* wise men die;
Likewise the fool and the senseless person perish,
And leave their wealth to others (Ps. 49:10).

The rich and the poor have this in common,
The LORD *is* the maker of them all (Prov. 22:2).

Remove falsehood and lies far from me;
Give me neither poverty nor riches—
Feed me with the food *You* prescribe for me; . . .
  (Prov. 30:8).

More to be desired *are they* than gold,
Yea, than much fine gold;
Sweeter also than honey and the honeycomb
  (Ps. 19:10).

Learn the Grace of Giving

Give to Others

"I have shown you in every way, by laboring like this, that you must support the weak. And remember the words of the Lord Jesus, that He

said, 'It is more blessed to give than to receive'"
(Acts 20:35).

There is *one* who scatters, yet increases more;
And there is *one* who withholds more than is right,
But it *leads* to poverty.
The generous soul will be made rich,
And he who waters will also be watered himself
    (Prov. 11:24–25).

A good *man* leaves an inheritance to his children's
    children,
But the wealth of the sinner is stored up for the
    righteous (Prov. 13:22).

He who has pity on the poor lends to the LORD,
And He will pay back what he has given
    (Prov. 19:17).

He who has a bountiful eye will be blessed,
For he gives of his bread to the poor (Prov. 22:9).

Cast your bread upon the waters,
For you will find it after many days (Eccles. 11:1).

"Give to everyone who asks of you. And from him
who takes away your goods do not ask *them* back"
(Luke 6:30).

Give to God
"Sell what you have and give alms; provide
yourselves money bags which do not grow old, a
treasure in the heavens that does not fail, where no

thief approaches nor moth destroys. For where your treasure is, there your heart will be also" (Luke 12:33–34).

Then He looked up and saw the rich putting their gifts into the treasury, and He saw also a certain poor widow putting in two mites. So He said, "Truly I say to you that this poor widow has put in more than all; for all these out of their abundance have put in offerings for God, but she out of her poverty has put in all the livelihood that she had" (Luke 21:1–4).

Moreover, brethren, we make known to you the grace of God bestowed on the churches of Macedonia: that in a great trial of affliction the abundance of their joy and their deep poverty abounded in the riches of their liberality. For I bear witness that according to *their* ability, yes, and beyond *their* ability, *they were* freely willing, imploring us with much urgency that we would receive the gift and the fellowship of the ministering to the saints. And *this they did,* not as we had hoped, but first gave themselves to the Lord, and *then* to us by the will of God. So we urged Titus, that as he had begun, so he would also complete this grace in you as well. But as you abound in everything—in faith, in speech, in knowledge, in all diligence, and in your love for us—*see* that you abound in this grace also (2 Cor. 8:1–7).

But this *I say:* He who sows sparingly will also reap sparingly, and he who sows bountifully will also reap bountifully. *So let* each one *give* as he purposes in his heart, not grudgingly or of necessity; for God loves a cheerful giver (2 Cor. 9:6–7).

Then the men turned away from there and went toward Sodom, but Abraham still stood before the LORD (Gen. 18:22).

'And all the tithe of the land, *whether* of the seed of the land *or* of the fruit of the tree, *is* the LORD's. It *is* holy to the LORD. . . . And concerning the tithe of the herd or the flock, of whatever passes under the rod, the tenth one shall be holy to the LORD'" (Lev. 27:30,32).

"Will a man rob God?
Yet you have robbed Me!
But you say,
'In what way have we robbed You?'
In tithes and offerings" (Mal. 3:8).

Now concerning the collection for the saints, as I have given orders to the churches of Galatia, so you must do also: On the first *day* of the week let each one of you lay something aside, storing up as he may prosper, that there be no collections when I come (1 Cor. 16:1–2).

═16═

Homemaking

Homemaking is the most honorable profession in the world. It is essential to the stability and perpetuity of the family. By keeping the home, we make it a place of beauty, rest and comfort for every family member. As such, the home ideally becomes a place of security and protection, as well as a place of learning and instruction in the things of God.

"Every wise woman builds her house," declares the writer of Proverbs (see 14:1). The godly woman ought to be concerned with every detail of family life and homemaking to the glory of God. From cleaning the house to doing the dishes, she is building a place of security for herself, her husband and her children.

Homemaking is not something that can be taken for granted. It takes diligence, persistence and consistency to build a home God's way. He must be the foundation, and we must build upon that foundation very carefully. Every quality of personal character and moral virtue is essential in the building of a home on the foundation of the solid rock: Jesus Christ.

The skills of cooking, cleaning, child discipline and time management are all essential ingredients to biblical homemaking. But above all else, the task of establishing a spiritual environment is the ultimate priority. As in constructing a house, building a "home" requires a blueprint of guidelines to follow. In this case they are found in the word of God.

Build Your Home on a Spiritual Foundation

Build Your Home Upon Christ

"Therefore whoever hears these sayings of Mine, and does them, I will liken him to a wise man who built his house on the rock: and the rain descended, the floods came, and the winds blew and beat on that house; and it did not fall, for it was founded on the rock. Now everyone who hears these sayings of Mine, and does not do them, will be like a foolish man who built his house on the sand: and the rain descended, the floods came, and the winds blew and beat on that house; and it fell. And great was its fall" (Matt. 7:24–27).

Build Your Home Upon Righteousness

The wicked are overthrown and *are* no more,
But the house of the righteous will stand
(Prov. 12:7).

The house of the wicked will be overthrown,
But the tent of the upright will flourish
(Prov. 14:11).

Build Your Home Upon Wisdom

Every wise woman builds her house,
But the foolish pulls it down with her hands
(Prov. 14:1).

Wisdom has built her house,
She has hewn out her seven pillars;
She has slaughtered her meat,
She has mixed her wine,
She has also furnished her table.
She has sent out her maidens,
She cries out from the highest places of the city,
"Whoever *is* simple, let him turn in here!"
As for him who lacks understanding, she says to
him,
"Come, eat of my bread
And drink of the wine *which* I have mixed.
Forsake foolishness and live;
And go in the way of understanding" (Prov. 9:1–6).

Build Your Home Upon Discretion

. . . that they admonish the young women to love
their husbands, to love their children, to be
discreet, chaste, homemakers, good, obedient to
their own husbands, that the word of God may not
be blasphemed (Titus 2:4–5).

Build Your Home Upon Unity

Behold, how good and how pleasant *it is*
For brethren to dwell together in unity! (Ps. 133:1).

But Jesus knew their thoughts, and said to them:
"Every kingdom divided against itself is brought to
desolation, and every city or house divided against
itself will not stand" (Matt. 12:25).

. . . and to esteem them very highly in love for
their work's sake. Be at peace among yourselves
(1 Thess. 5:13).

Homemaking Is an Important Calling

A Wife's Calling

Likewise *you* wives, *be* submissive to your own
husbands, that even if some do not obey the word,
they, without a word, may be won by the conduct
of their wives, when they observe your chaste
conduct *accompanied* by fear. Do not let your beauty
be that outward *adorning* of arranging the hair, of
wearing gold, or of putting on *fine* apparel; but *let it
be* the hidden person of the heart, with the
incorruptible *ornament* of a gentle and quiet spirit,
which is very precious in the sight of God
(1 Pet. 3:1–4).

Her Great Value

Houses and riches *are* an inheritance from fathers,
But a prudent wife *is* from the LORD (Prov. 19:14).

Who can find a virtuous wife?
For her worth *is* far above rubies (Prov. 31:10).

She Honors Her Husband

An excellent wife *is* the crown of her husband,
But she who causes shame *is* like rottenness in his
   bones (Prov. 12:4).

The heart of her husband safely trusts her;
So he will have no lack of gain.
She does him good and not evil
All the days of her life (Prov. 31:11–12).

Her husband is known in the gates,
When he sits among the elders of the land
   (Prov. 31:23).

She Is Talented

She seeks wool and flax,
And willingly works with her hands.
She is like the merchant ships,
She brings her food from afar.
She also rises while it is yet night,
And provides food for her household,
And a portion for her maidservants.
She considers a field and buys it;
From her profits she plants a vineyard.
She girds herself with strength,
And strengthens her arms.
She perceives that her merchandise *is* good,
And her lamp does not go out by night.

She stretches out her hands to the distaff,
And her hand holds the spindle (Prov. 31:13–19).

She Is Generous

She extends her hand to the poor,
Yes, she reaches out her hands to the needy.
She is not afraid of snow for her household,
For all her household *is* clothed with scarlet.
She makes tapestry for herself;
Her clothing *is* fine linen and purple
   (Prov. 31:20–22).

She Is Honorable

A gracious woman retains honor,
But ruthless *men* retain riches (Prov. 11:16).

Strength and honor *are* her clothing;
She shall rejoice in time to come (Prov. 31:25).

She Is Wise

She opens her mouth with wisdom,
And on her tongue *is* the law of kindness
   (Prov. 31:26).

She Is Industrious

She watches over the ways of her household,
And does not eat the bread of idleness (Prov. 31:27).

She Is Blessed

Her children rise up and call her blessed;
Her husband *also*, and he praises her:

"Many daughters have done well,
But you excel them all."
Charm *is* deceitful and beauty *is* vain,
But a woman *who* fears the LORD, she shall be
    praised.
Give her of the fruit of her hands,
And let her own works praise her in the gates
    (Prov. 31:28–31).

Qualities of an Ideal Home

Love

And now abide faith, hope, love, these three; but
the greatest of these *is* love (1 Cor. 13:13).

Though I speak with the tongues of men and of
angels, but have not love, I have become *as*
sounding brass or a clanging cymbal (1 Cor. 13:1).

Humility

When pride comes, then comes shame;
But with the humble *is* wisdom (Prov. 11:2).

The fear of the LORD *is* the instruction of wisdom,
And before honor *is* humility (Prov. 15:33).

Self-Control

Keep your heart with all diligence,
For out of it *spring* the issues of life.
Put away from you a deceitful mouth,
And put perverse lips far from you.
Let your eyes look straight ahead,
And your eyelids look right before you.

Ponder the path of your feet,
And let all your ways be established.
Do not turn to the right or the left;
Remove your foot from evil (Prov. 4:23–27).

When you sit down to eat with a ruler,
Consider carefully what *is* before you:
And put a knife to your throat
If you *are* a man given to appetite.
Do not desire his delicacies,
For they *are* deceptive (Prov. 23:1–3).

Whoever *has* no rule over his own spirit
Is like a city broken down, without walls
    (Prov. 25:28).

Strength

In the fear of the LORD *there is* strong confidence,
And *His* children will have a place of refuge
    (Prov. 14:26).

The way of the LORD *is* strength for the upright,
But destruction *will come* to the workers of iniquity
    (Prov. 10:29).

A wise man *is* strong,
Yes, a man of knowledge increases strength; . . .
    (Prov. 24:5).

Righteousness

When the whirlwind passes by, the wicked *is* no
    more,
But the righteous *has* an everlasting foundation.

209

As vinegar to the teeth and smoke to the eyes,
So *is* the sluggard to those who send him.
The fear of the LORD prolongs days,
But the years of the wicked will be shortened.
The hope of the righteous *will be* gladness,
But the expectation of the wicked will perish
  (Prov. 10:25–28).

A wicked man hardens his face,
But *as for* the upright, he establishes his way
  (Prov. 21:29).

The name of the LORD *is* a strong tower;
The righteous run to it and are safe (Prov. 18:10).

The righteous eats to the satisfying of his soul,
But the stomach of the wicked shall be in want
  (Prov. 13:25).

In the way of righteousness *is* life,
And in *its* pathway *there is* no death (Prov. 12:28).

Peace
Better *is* a dry morsel with quietness,
Than a house full of feasting *with* strife (Prov. 17:1).

Better *is* a little with the fear of the LORD,
Than great treasure with trouble.
Better *is* a dinner of herbs where love is,
Than a fatted calf with hatred (Prov. 15:16–17).

. . . and the peace of God, which surpasses all
understanding, will guard your hearts and minds
through Christ Jesus. . . . The things which you

learned and received and heard and saw in me,'
these do, and the God of peace will be with you
(Phil. 4:7,9).

Integrity

The righteous *man* walks in his integrity;
His children *are* blessed after him (Prov. 20:7).

Praise the LORD!
Blessed *is* the man *who* fears the LORD,
Who delights greatly in His commandments.
His descendants will be mighty on earth;
The generation of the upright will be blessed.
Wealth and riches *will be* in his house,
And his righteousness endures forever
(Ps. 112:1–3).

Blessed *is* every one who fears the LORD,
Who walks in His ways.
When you eat the labor of your hands,
You *shall be* happy and *it shall be* well with you.
Your wife *shall be* like a fruitful vine
In the very heart of your house,
Your children like olive plants
All around your table.
Behold, thus shall the man be blessed
Who fears the LORD (Ps. 128:1–4).

Diligence

Do not look upon me, because I *am* dark,
Because the sun has tanned me.
My mother's sons were angry with me;

They made me the keeper of the vineyards,
But my own vineyard I have not kept
   (Song of Sol. 1:6).

"When an unclean spirit goes out of a man, he goes through dry places, seeking rest; and finding none, he says, 'I will return to my house from which I came.' And when he comes, he finds *it* swept and put in order. Then he goes and takes with *him* seven other spirits more wicked than himself, and they enter and dwell there; and the last *state* of that man is worse than the first" (Luke 11:24–26).

Worship

For a day in Your courts *is* better than a thousand.
I would rather be a doorkeeper in the house of my
   God
Than dwell in the tents of wickedness (Ps. 84:10).

. . . to the beloved Apphia, Archippus our fellow soldier, and to the church in your house: . . . (Philem. 1:2).

Greet Priscilla and Aquila, my fellow workers in Christ Jesus, who risked their own necks for my life, to whom not only I give thanks, but also all the churches of the Gentiles. Likewise *greet* the church that is in their house. Greet my beloved Epaenetus, who is the firstfruits of Achaia to Christ (Rom. 16:3–5).

Therefore, as we have opportunity, let us do good to all, especially to those who are of the household of faith (Gal. 6:10).

. . . you also, as living stones, are being built up a spiritual house, a holy priesthood, to offer up spiritual sacrifices acceptable to God through Jesus Christ (1 Pet. 2:5).

═══ 17 ═══

Widows and Orphans

God helps the helpless. The Bible states that He is a "Father to the fatherless." Widows and orphans especially are under His care. In the Old Testament, the Law protected them. In the New Testament, the Church cared for them. The apostle James went so far as to say: "Pure and undefiled religion before God and the Father is this: to visit orphans and widows in their trouble" (James 1:27).

Jesus commended the widow who gave all her substance above the rich who gave out of their abundance (see Mark 12:41–44). The prophet Elijah was ministered to by a widow in Zeraphath in Phoenicia, who gave to him by faith out of her poverty. Later, the prophet raised her son from the dead in appreciation for all she had done for him (see 1 Kings 17:8–24).

We are never so alone that God is not with us. We are never so destitute that He cannot provide. We are never so helpless that He cannot help us. We are never so needy that He cannot meet our needs. Trust Him, for He cares for you.

God's Law Protected Widows and Orphans

God Hears Their Cry

"You shall not afflict any widow or fatherless child. If you afflict them in any way, *and* they cry at all to Me, I will surely hear their cry; and My wrath will become hot, and I will kill you with the sword; your wives shall be widows, and your children fatherless" (Exod. 22:22–24).

"'Do not oppress the widow or the fatherless,
The alien or the poor.
Let none of you plan evil in his heart
Against his brother'" (Zech. 7:10).

God Loves Widows and Orphans

"For the LORD your God *is* God of gods and Lord of lords, the great God, mighty and awesome, who shows no partiality nor takes a bribe. He administers justice for the fatherless and the widow, and loves the stranger, giving him food and clothing" (Deut. 10:17–18).

God Helps Widows and Orphans

But You have seen *it*, for
    You observe trouble and grief,
To repay *it* by Your hand.
The helpless commits himself to You;
You are the helper of the fatherless (Ps. 10:14).

215

The LORD watches over the strangers;
He relieves the fatherless and widow;
But the way of the wicked He turns upside down
    (Ps. 146:9).

God Cares for Widows and Orphans

A father of the fatherless, a defender of widows,
Is God in His holy habitation (Ps. 68:5).

"Assyria shall not save us,
We will not ride on horses,
Nor will we say anymore to the work of our hands,
'You *are* our gods.'
For in You the fatherless finds mercy" (Hos. 14:3).

"Leave your fatherless children,
I will preserve *them* alive;
And let your widows trust in Me" (Jer. 49:11).

He Causes Them to Rejoice

Because I delivered the poor who cried out,
And the fatherless and *he who had* no helper.
The blessing of a perishing *man* came upon me,
And I caused the widow's heart to sing for joy
    (Job 29:12–13).

God Delivers Them from Trouble

For He will deliver the needy when he cries,
The poor also, and *him* who has no helper.
He will spare the poor and needy,
And will save the souls of the needy.

He will redeem their life from oppression and
   violence;
And precious shall be their blood in His sight
   (Ps. 72:12–14).

To do justice to the fatherless and the oppressed,
That the man of the earth may oppress no more
   (Ps. 10:18).

We Are to Care for Widows and Orphans

Defend Them

Defend the poor and fatherless;
Do justice to the afflicted and needy (Ps. 82:3).

"For if you thoroughly amend your ways and your
doings, if you thoroughly execute judgment
between a man and his neighbor, *if* you do not
oppress the stranger, the fatherless, and the widow,
and do not shed innocent blood in this place, or
walk after other gods to your hurt, then I will cause
you to dwell in this place, in the land that I gave to
your fathers forever and ever" (Jer. 7:5–7).

Learn to do good;
Seek justice,
Reprove the oppressor;
Defend the fatherless,
Plead for the widow (Isa. 1:17).

" 'Cursed *is* the one who perverts the justice due
the stranger, the fatherless, and widow.' And all the
people shall say, 'Amen!' " (Deut. 27:19).

"And I will come near you for judgment;
I will be a swift witness
Against sorcerers,
Against adulterers,
Against perjurers,
Against those who exploit wage earners and
    widows and the fatherless,
And against those who turn away an alien—
Because they do not fear Me,"
Says the LORD of hosts. (Mal. 3:5).

"Woe to you, scribes and Pharisees, hypocrites! For you devour widows' houses, and for a pretense make long prayers. Therefore you will receive greater condemnation" (Matt. 23:14).

Provide for Them
"At the end of *every* third year you shall bring out the tithe of your produce of that year and store *it* up within your gates. And the Levite, because he has no portion nor inheritance with you, and the stranger and the fatherless and the widow who *are* within your gates, may come and eat and be satisfied, that the LORD your God may bless you in all the work of your hand which you do" (Deut. 14:28–29).

"And *take heed*, lest you lift your eyes to heaven, and *when* you see the sun, the moon, and the stars, all the host of heaven, you feel driven to worship them and serve them, which the LORD your God has given to all the peoples under the whole heaven as a heritage. But the LORD has taken you and brought you out of the iron furnace, out of Egypt, to be His people, *His* inheritance, as you are this day. Furthermore the LORD was angry with me for your sakes, and swore that I would not cross over the Jordan, and that I would not enter the good land which the LORD your God is giving you as an inheritance" (Deut. 4:19–21).

"When you have finished laying aside all the tithe of your increase in the third year, *which is* the year of tithing, and have given *it* to the Levite, the stranger, the fatherless, and the widow, so that they may eat within your gates and be filled, then you shall say before the LORD your God: 'I have removed the holy *tithe* from *my* house and also have given them to the Levite, the stranger, the fatherless, and the widow, according to all Your commandments which You have commanded me; I have not transgressed Your commandments, nor have I forgotten *them*'" (Deut. 26:12–13).

Now in those days, when *the number of* the disciples was multiplying, there arose a murmuring against the Hebrews by the Hellenists, because their widows were neglected in the daily distribution. Then the twelve summoned the multitude of the disciples and said, "It is not desirable that we should leave the word of God and serve tables. Therefore, brethren, seek out from among you seven men of *good* reputation, full of the Holy Spirit

219

and wisdom, whom we may appoint over this business; . . . (Acts 6:1–3).

Honor Widows and Orphans

"You shall rejoice before the LORD your God, you and your son and your daughter, your manservant and your maidservant, the Levite who *is* within your gates, the stranger and the fatherless and the widow who *are* among you, at the place where the LORD your God chooses to make His name abide. . . . and you shall rejoice in your feast, you and your son and your daughter, your manservant and your maidservant and the Levite, the stranger and the fatherless and the widow, who *are* within your gates" (Deut. 16:11,14).

Honor widows who are really widows (1 Tim. 5:3).

Visit Widows and Orphans

Pure and undefiled religion before God and the Father is this: to visit orphans and widows in their trouble, *and* to keep oneself unspotted from the world (James 1:27).

Widows Are also Responsible for Themselves

Widows Are Responsible for Their Decisions

"But any vow of a widow or a divorced woman, by which she has bound herself, shall stand against her" (Num. 30:9)

Widows and Orphans

Widows Can Remarry

But I say to the unmarried and the widows: It is good for them if they remain even as I am; but if they cannot exercise self-control, let them marry. For it is better to marry than to burn *with passion* (1 Cor. 7:8–9).

Therefore I desire that *the* younger *widows* marry, bear children, manage the house, give no opportunity to the adversary to speak reproachfully (1 Tim. 5:14).

Widows Can Minister to Others

Then the word of the LORD came to him, saying, "Arise, go to Zarephath, which *belongs* to Sidon, and dwell there. See, I have commanded a widow there to provide for you" (1 Kings 17:8–9).

Now Jesus sat opposite the treasury and saw how the people put money into the treasury. And many *who were* rich put in much. Then one poor widow came and threw in two mites, which make a quadrans. So He called His disciples *to Him* and said to them, "Assuredly, I say to you that this poor widow has put in more than all those who have given to the treasury; for they all put in out of their abundance, but she out of her poverty put in all that she had, her whole livelihood" (Mark 12:41–44).

The Church's Care for Widows

Some Widows Have Children to Care For Them

But if any widow has children or grandchildren,
let them first learn to show piety at home and
to repay their parents; for this is good and
acceptable before God (1 Tim. 5:4).

Some Widows Are Destitute

Now she who is really a widow, and left alone,
trusts in God and continues in supplications and
prayers night and day (1 Tim. 5:5).

Some Widows Have Family to Care for Them

But if anyone does not provide for his own, and
especially for those of his household, he has denied
the faith and is worse than an unbeliever. . . . If
any believing man or woman has widows, let them
relieve them, and do not let the church be
burdened, that it may relieve those who are really
widows (1 Tim. 5:8,16).

Some Widows Are Living in Sin

But she who lives in pleasure is dead while she
lives. And these things command, that they may be
blameless. . . . But refuse *the* younger widows; for
when they have begun to grow wanton against
Christ, they desire to marry, having condemnation
because they have cast off their first faith. And
besides they learn *to be* idle, wandering about from
house to house, and not only idle but also gossips

and busybodies, saying things which they ought not (1 Tim. 5:6,7,11–13).

Younger Widows Should Remarry

Therefore I desire that *the* younger *widows* marry, bear children, manage the house, give no opportunity to the adversary to speak reproachfully (1 Tim. 5:14).

Destitute Older Widows Are Under Church Care

Honor widows who are really widows. . . . Now she who is really a widow, and left alone, trusts in God and continues in supplications and prayers night and day (1 Tim. 5:3,5).

Do not let a widow under sixty years old be taken into the number, *and not unless* she has been the wife of one man, well reported for good works: if she has brought up children, if she has lodged strangers, if she has washed the saints' feet, if she has relieved the afflicted, if she has diligently followed every good work. . . . If any believing man or woman has widows, let them relieve them, and do not let the church be burdened, that it may relieve those who are really widows (1 Tim. 5:9–10,16).

═18═

Hospitality

Examples of hospitality abound throughout the Bible. In both the Old and New Testaments, godly people cared for one another. They opened their homes to relatives, friends and strangers alike. In some cases, they even "unwittingly entertained angels" (Heb. 13:2).

Acts of hospitality illustrated in Scripture include the provision of food, shelter, clothing, money, protection, advice and, in some cases, a wife. In the ancient Near East, hospitality was considered one of the highest virtues among the desert cultures. Among the Israelites it was highly esteemed because they had once been in bondage in a strange land. Thus, their hearts went out to strangers and to the oppressed.

Hospitality is an expression of the gift of serving (see Romans 12:10). It is an act of generosity that involves sharing the good provisions of God with others. The more you learn to share, the more you will want to share. As you give of yourself and your home to others, you will indeed be sharing the love of Christ with them.

Hospitality Is Commended by God

God Cares for Those in Need

"For the LORD your God *is* God of gods and Lord of lords, the great God, mighty and awesome, who shows no partiality nor takes a bribe. He administers justice for the fatherless and the widow, and loves the stranger, giving him food and clothing" (Deut. 10:17,18).

Therefore your gates shall be open continually;
They shall not be shut day or night,
That *men* may bring to you the wealth of the
   Gentiles,
And their kings in procession (Isa. 60:11).

He Asks Us to Care Also

"'. . . for I was hungry and you gave Me food; I was thirsty and you gave Me drink; I was a stranger and you took Me in; 'I *was* naked and you clothed Me; I was sick and you visited Me; I was in prison and you came to Me.' Then the righteous will answer Him, saying, 'Lord, when did we see You hungry and feed *You,* or thirsty and give *You* drink? When did we see You a stranger and take *You* in, or naked and clothe *You*? Or when did we see You sick, or in prison, and come to You?' And the King will answer and say to them, 'Assuredly, I say to you, inasmuch as you did *it* to one of the least of these My brethren, you did *it* to Me'" (Matt. 25:35–40).

225

Then He also said to him who invited Him, "When you give a dinner or a supper, do not ask your friends, your brothers, your relatives, nor *your* rich neighbors, lest they also invite you back, and you be repaid. But when you give a feast, invite *the* poor, *the* maimed, *the* lame, *the* blind. And you will be blessed, because they cannot repay you; for you shall be repaid at the resurrection of the just" (Luke 14:12–14).

Therefore receive one another, just as Christ also received us, to the glory of God (Rom. 15:7).

Hospitality Is a Virtue
"The LORD repay your work, and a full reward be given you by the LORD God of Israel, under whose wings you have come for refuge." Then she said, "Let me find favor in your sight, my lord; for you have comforted me, and have spoken kindly to your maidservant, though I am not like one of your maidservants." Now Boaz said to her at mealtime, "Come here, and eat of the bread, and dip your piece of the bread in the vinegar." So she sat beside the reapers, and he passed parched *grain* to her; and she ate and was satisfied, and kept some back. And when she rose up to glean, Boaz commanded his young men, saying, "Let her glean even among the sheaves, and do not reproach her. Also let *some grain* from the bundles fall purposely for her; leave *it* that she may glean, and do not rebuke her" (Ruth 2:12–16).

. . . well reported for good works: if she has brought up children, if she has lodged strangers, if she has washed the saints' feet, if she has relieved the afflicted, if she has diligently followed every good work (1 Tim. 5:10).

. . . but hospitable, a lover of what is good, sober-minded, just, holy, self-controlled, . . . (Titus 1:8).

Do not forget to entertain strangers, for by so *doing* some have unwittingly entertained angels (Heb. 13:2).

Hospitality Is a Blessing

Then she fell on her face, bowed down to the ground, and said to him, "Why have I found favor in your eyes, that you should take notice of me, since I *am* a foreigner?" (Ruth 2:10).

Then Paul dwelt two whole years in his own rented house, and received all who came to him, . . . (Acts 28:30).

. . . distributing to the needs of the saints, given to hospitality (Rom. 12:13).

Repay no one evil for evil. Have regard for good things in the sight of all men. If it is possible, as much as depends on you, live peaceably with all men. Beloved, do not avenge yourselves, but *rather* give place to wrath; for it is written, *"Vengeance is Mine, I will repay,"* says the Lord.

"Therefore if your enemy hungers, feed him;
If he thirsts, give him a drink;
For in so doing you will heap coals of fire on his head."

Do not be overcome by evil, but overcome evil with good (Rom. 12:17–21).

Be hospitable to one another without grumbling (1 Pet. 4:9).

Do not let a widow under sixty years old be taken into the number, *and not unless* she has been the wife of one man, well reported for good works: if she has brought up children, if she has lodged strangers, if she has washed the saints' feet, if she has relieved the afflicted, if she has diligently followed every good work (1 Tim. 5:9–10).

Hospitality Has Its Limits

Seldom set foot in your neighbor's house,
Lest he become weary of you and hate you
    (Prov. 25:17).

A continual dripping on a very rainy day
And a contentious woman are alike; . . . .
    (Prov. 27:15).

And put a knife to your throat
If you *are* a man given to appetite (Prov. 23:2).

Hospitality

Hospitality Wins Friends and Influences People

Example of Abraham

Then the LORD appeared to him by the terebinth trees of Mamre, as he was sitting in the tent door in the heat of the day. So he lifted his eyes and looked, and behold, three men were standing by him; and when he saw *them*, he ran from the tent door to meet them, and bowed himself to the ground, and said, "My Lord, if I have now found favor in Your sight, do not pass on by Your servant. Please let a little water be brought and wash your feet, and rest yourselves under the tree. And I will bring a morsel of bread, that you may refresh your hearts. After that you may pass by, inasmuch as you have come to your servant." And they said, "Do as you have said." So Abraham hastened into the tent to Sarah and said, "Quickly, make ready three measures of fine meal; knead *it* and make cakes." And Abraham ran to the herd, took a tender and good calf, gave it to a young man, and he hastened to prepare it. So he took butter and milk and the calf which he had prepared, and set *it* before them; and he stood by them under the tree as they ate (Gen. 18:1–8).

Example of Lot

Now the two angels came to Sodom in the evening, and Lot was sitting in the gate of Sodom. When Lot saw *them*, he rose to meet them, and he bowed himself with his face toward the ground. And he said, "Here now, my lords, please turn in to your servant's house and spend the night, and wash your feet; then you may rise early and go on your way." And they said, "No, but we will spend the night in the open square." But he insisted strongly; so they turned in to him and entered his house. Then he made them a feast, and baked unleavened bread, and they ate (Gen. 19:1–3).

Example of Laban
And he said, "Come in, O blessed of the LORD! Why do you stand outside? For I have prepared the house, and a place for the camels." Then the man came to the house. And he unloaded the camels, and provided straw and feed for the camels, and water to wash his feet and the feet of the men who *were* with him (Gen. 24:31–32).

Example of Abigail
Then Abigail made haste and took two hundred *loaves* of bread, two skins of wine, five sheep already dressed, five seahs of roasted *grain*, one hundred clusters of raisins, and two hundred cakes of figs, and loaded *them* on donkeys. . . . Now when Abigail saw David, she hastened to dismount from the donkey, fell on her face before David, and bowed down to the ground. . . . "And now this present which your maidservant has brought to my lord, let it be given to the young men who followed my lord. . . ." Then David said to Abigail: "Blessed

be the LORD God of Israel, who sent you this day to meet me!" (1 Sam. 25:18,23,27,32).

Example of the Widow

"Arise, go to Zarephath, which *belongs* to Sidon, and dwell there. See, I have commanded a widow there to provide for you." So he arose and went to Zarephath. And when he came to the gate of the city, indeed a widow *was* there gathering sticks. And he called to her and said, "Please bring me a little water in a cup, that I may drink. For thus says the LORD God of Israel: 'The bin of flour shall not be used up, nor shall the jar of oil run dry, until the day the LORD sends rain on the earth'"
(1 Kings 17:9,10,14).

Example of Mary and Martha

Now Jesus loved Martha and her sister and Lazarus (John 11:5).

There they made Him a supper; and Martha served, but Lazarus was one of those who sat at the table with Him. Then Mary took a pound of very costly oil of spikenard, anointed the feet of Jesus, and wiped His feet with her hair. And the house was filled with the fragrance of the oil (John 12:2–3).

Now it happened as they went that He entered a certain village; and a certain woman named Martha welcomed Him into her house. And she had a sister called Mary, who also sat at Jesus' feet and heard His word. But Martha was distracted with much serving, and she approached Him and said, "Lord, do You not care that my sister has left me to serve alone? Therefore tell her to help me." And Jesus answered and said to her, "Martha, Martha, you are worried and troubled about many things. But one thing is needed, and Mary has chosen that good part, which will not be taken away from her" (Luke 10:38–42).

Example of Lydia
And when she and her household were baptized, she begged *us*, saying, "If you have judged me to be faithful to the Lord, come to my house and stay." And she constrained us (Acts 16:15).

Example of the Philippian Jailor
And he took them the same hour of the night and washed *their* stripes. And immediately he and all his family were baptized. Now when he had brought them into his house, he set food before them; and he rejoiced, having believed in God with all his household (Acts 16:33–34).

Example of Philip the Evangelist
On the next *day* we who were Paul's companions departed and came to Caesarea, and entered the house of Philip the evangelist, who was *one* of the seven, and stayed with him (Acts 21:8).

Hospitality

Example of Paul

Then Paul dwelt two whole years in his own rented house, and received all who came to him, preaching the kingdom of God and teaching the things which concern the Lord Jesus Christ with all confidence, no one forbidding him (Acts 2:30–31).

Example of Paul...

══ 19 ══

Church

The Church of Jesus Christ is God's institution on earth to preach the gospel of salvation and point men toward heaven. For the Christian family, the Church is the central place of worship and personal ministry to each family member. Our involvement in the regular functions of the Church is a consistent example and constant reminder to our children about the importance of the things of God.

The local Church is the place where the family worships together. It is the place where we seek God's guidance and blessing in our own lives. It is also the place where we can have an active part in the ministry of the Church as we reach out to others in need.

Active Church involvement is a vital sign of a happy and healthy Christian family. Participation in the life and ministry of the Church is an expression of our love and devotion to God. The Scripture encourages us not to forsake "the assembling of ourselves together" (Heb. 10:25). Regular and consistent attendance indicates the depth of our commitment. It also reveals the genuineness of our concern for others.

Every family needs to attend a Bible-believing and preaching Church for its regular services. Get involved and volunteer for service. Find areas where you can help out and do it to the glory of God. You will be glad you did. As the apostle Paul wrote: "To Him be glory in the Church by Christ Jesus throughout all ages, world without end. Amen." (Eph. 3:21).

Nature of the Church

Founded by Jesus Christ

When Jesus came into the region of Caesarea Philippi, He asked His disciples, saying, "Who do men say that I, the Son of Man, am? . . ." And Simon Peter answered and said, "You are the Christ, the Son of the living God." Jesus answered and said to him, "Blessed are you, Simon Bar-Jonah, for flesh and blood has not revealed *this* to you, but My Father who is in heaven. And I also say to you that you are Peter, and on this rock I will build My church, and the gates of Hades shall not prevail against it" (Matt. 16:13,16–18).

. . . which He worked in Christ when He raised Him from the dead and seated *Him* at His right hand in the heavenly *places,* far above all principality and power and might and dominion, and every name that is named, not only in this age but also in that which is to come. And He put all *things* under His feet, and gave Him *to be* head over all *things* to the church, which is His body, the fullness of Him who fills all in all (Eph. 1:20–23).

Unique People of God

But you *are* a chosen generation, a royal priesthood, a holy nation, His own special people, that you may proclaim the praises of Him who called you out of darkness into His marvelous light; who once *were* not a people but *are* now the people of God, who had not obtained mercy but now have obtained mercy (1 Pet. 2:9–10).

Do not be unequally yoked together with unbelievers. For what fellowship has righteousness with lawlessness? And what communion has light with darkness? And what accord has Christ with Belial? Or what part has a believer with an unbeliever? And what agreement has the temple of God with idols? For you are the temple of the living God. As God has said:

> "I will dwell in them
> And walk among them.
> I will be their God,
> And they shall be My people"
> (2 Cor. 6:14–16).

An Assembly of Believers

. . . elect according to the foreknowledge of God the Father, in sanctification of the Spirit, for

obedience and sprinkling of the blood of Jesus
Christ: Grace to you and peace be multiplied.
Blessed *be* the God and Father of our Lord Jesus
Christ, who according to His abundant mercy has
begotten us again to a living hope through the
resurrection of Jesus Christ from the dead, . . .
(1 Pet. 1:2–3).

And thus the secrets of his heart are revealed; and
so, falling down on *his* face, he will worship God
and report that God is truly among you
(1 Cor. 14:25).

But if I am delayed, *I write* so that you may know
how you ought to conduct yourself in the house of
God, which is the church of the living God, the
pillar and ground of the truth (1 Tim. 3:15).

Citizens of Heaven

But now in Christ Jesus you who once were far off
have been made near by the blood of Christ. For He
Himself is our peace, who has made both one, and
has broken down the middle wall of division
between us, having abolished in His flesh the
enmity, *that is,* the law of commandments *contained*
in ordinances, so as to create in Himself one new
man *from* the two, *thus* making peace, and that He
might reconcile them both to God in one body
through the cross, thereby putting to death the
enmity. And He came and preached peace to you
who were afar off and to those who were near. For
through Him we both have access by one Spirit to

the Father. Now, therefore, you are no longer
strangers and foreigners, but fellow citizens with
the saints and members of the household of God,
having been built on the foundation of the apostles
and prophets, Jesus Christ Himself being the chief
cornerstone, in whom the whole building, being
joined together, grows into a holy temple in the
Lord, in whom you also are being built together for
a habitation of God in the Spirit (Eph. 2:13–22).

Temple of God

For we are God's fellow workers; you are God's
field, *you are* God's building. According to the grace
of God which was given to me, as a wise master
builder I have laid the foundation, and another
builds on it. But let each one take heed how he
builds on it. For no other foundation can anyone lay
than that which is laid, which is Jesus Christ. . . .
Do you not know that you are the temple of God
and *that* the Spirit of God dwells in you?
(1 Cor. 3:9–11,16).

Or do you not know that your body is the temple
of the Holy Spirit *who is* in you, whom you have
from God, and you are not your own? For you were
bought at a price; therefore glorify God in your
body and in your spirit, which are God's
(1 Cor. 6:19–20).

. . . you also, as living stones, are being built up a
spiritual house, a holy priesthood, to offer up
spiritual sacrifices acceptable to God through Jesus

Christ. Therefore it is also contained in the Scripture,

> "Behold, I lay in Zion
> A chief cornerstone, elect, precious,
> And he who believes on Him will by no means be put to shame."

Therefore, to you who believe, *He is* precious; but to those who are disobedient,

> "The stone which the builders rejected
> Has become the chief cornerstone," . . .
> (1 Pet. 2:5–7).

Body of Christ

For as the body is one and has many members, but all the members of that one body, being many, are one body, so also *is* Christ. For by one Spirit we were all baptized into one body—whether Jews or Greeks, whether slaves or free—and have all been made to drink into one Spirit. . . . Now you are the body of Christ, and members individually (1 Cor. 12:12–13,27).

For you are all sons of God through faith in Christ Jesus. For as many of you as were baptized into Christ have put on Christ. There is neither Jew nor Greek, there is neither slave nor free, there is neither male nor female; for you are all one in Christ Jesus (Gal. 3:26–28).

239

And He is the head of the body, the church, who is the beginning, the firstborn from the dead, that in all things He may have the preeminence. . . . And let the peace of God rule in your hearts, to which also you were called in one body; and be thankful (Col. 1:18; 3:15).

Flock of God

Shepherd the flock of God which is among you, serving as overseers, not by constraint but willingly, not for dishonest gain but eagerly; nor as being lords over those entrusted to you, but being examples to the flock; and when the Chief Shepherd appears, you will receive the crown of glory that does not fade away (1 Pet. 5:2–4).

"I am the good shepherd. The good shepherd gives His life for the sheep. . . . I am the good shepherd; and I know My *sheep,* and am known by My own. . . . My sheep hear My voice, and I know them, and they follow Me. And I give them eternal life, and they shall never perish; neither shall anyone snatch them out of My hand" (John 10:11,14,27–28).

Kingdom of Christ

He has delivered us from the power of darkness and translated *us* into the kingdom of the Son of His love, . . . (Col. 1:13).

. . . for the kingdom of God is not food and drink, but righteousness and peace and joy in the Holy Spirit (Rom. 14:17).

Bride of Christ

Husbands, love your wives, just as Christ also loved the church and gave Himself for it, that He might sanctify and cleanse it with the washing of water by the word, that He might present it to Himself a glorious church, not having spot or wrinkle or any such thing, but that it should be holy and without blemish. This is a great mystery, but I speak concerning Christ and the church (Eph. 5:25–27,32).

Then one of the seven angels who had the seven bowls filled with the seven last plagues came to me and talked with me, saying, "Come, I will show you the bride, the Lamb's wife." And he carried me away in the Spirit to a great and high mountain, and showed me the great city, the holy Jerusalem, descending out of heaven from God, having the glory of God (Rev. 21:9–11).

Ministry of the Church

Evangelism

Then Jesus came and spoke to them, saying, "All authority has been given to Me in heaven and on earth. Go therefore and make disciples of all the nations, baptizing them in the name of the Father and of the Son and of the Holy Spirit, teaching them to observe all things that I have commanded you; and lo, I am with you always, *even* to the end of the age." Amen (Matt. 28:18–20).

And He said to them, "Go into all the world and preach the gospel to every creature" (Mark 16:15).

Then He said to them, "Thus it is written, and thus it was necessary for the Christ to suffer and to rise from the dead the third day, and that repentance and remission of sins should be preached in His name to all nations, beginning at Jerusalem. And you are witnesses of these things" (Luke 24:46–48).

"But you shall receive power when the Holy Spirit has come upon you; and you shall be witnesses to Me in Jerusalem, and in all Judea and Samaria, and to the end of the earth" (Acts 1:8).

Edification

Then the churches throughout all Judea, Galilee, and Samaria had peace and were edified. And walking in the fear of the Lord and in the comfort of the Holy Spirit, they were multiplied (Acts 9:31).

Again do you think that we excuse ourselves to you? We speak before God in Christ. But *we do* all things, beloved, for your edification (2 Cor. 12:19).

Therefore I write these things being absent, lest being present I should use sharpness, according to the authority which the Lord has given me for edification and not for destruction. Finally, brethren, farewell. Become complete. Be of good comfort, be of one mind, live in peace; and the God of love and peace will be with you (2 Cor. 13:10–11).

Therefore let us pursue the things *which make* for peace and the things by which one may edify another (Rom. 14:19).

Therefore comfort each other and edify one another, just as you also are doing (1 Thess. 5:11).

And He Himself gave some *to be* apostles, some prophets, some evangelists, and some pastors and teachers, for the equipping of the saints for the work of ministry, for the edifying of the body of Christ, . . . (Eph. 4:11–12).

Fellowship

And they continued steadfastly in the apostles' doctrine and fellowship, in the breaking of bread, and in prayers. . . . So continuing daily with one accord in the temple, and breaking bread from house to house, they ate their food with gladness and simplicity of heart, praising God and having favor with all the people. And the Lord added to the church daily those who were being saved (Acts 2:42,46–47).

Now the multitude of those who believed were of one heart and one soul; neither did anyone say that any of the things he possessed was his own, but they had all things in common (Acts 4:32).

And daily in the temple, and in every house, they did not cease teaching and preaching Jesus *as* the Christ (Acts 5:42).

. . . for your fellowship in the gospel from the first day until now, . . . (Phil. 1:5).

. . . that I may know Him and the power of His resurrection, and the fellowship of His sufferings, being conformed to His death, . . (Phil. 3:10).

God *is* faithful, by whom you were called into the fellowship of His Son, Jesus Christ our Lord (1 Cor. 1:9).

. . . that which we have seen and heard we declare to you, that you also may have fellowship with us; and truly our fellowship *is* with the Father and with His Son Jesus Christ. . . . If we say that we have fellowship with Him, and walk in darkness, we lie and do not practice the truth. But if we walk in the light as He is in the light, we have fellowship with one another, and the blood of Jesus Christ His Son cleanses us from all sin (1 John 1:3,6–7).

Worship
Then Jesus said to him, "Away with you, Satan! For it is written, *'You shall worship the* LORD *your God, and Him only you shall serve'"* (Matt. 4:10).

"But the hour is coming, and now is, when the true worshipers will worship the Father in spirit and truth; for the Father is seeking such to worship

Him. God *is* Spirit, and those who worship Him must worship in spirit and truth" (John 4:23–24).

And thus the secrets of his heart are revealed; and so, falling down on *his* face, he will worship God and report that God is truly among you (1 Cor. 14:25).

For we are the circumcision, who worship God in the Spirit, rejoice in Christ Jesus, and have no confidence in the flesh, . . . (Phil. 3:3).

. . . the twenty-four elders fall down before Him who sits on the throne and worship Him who lives forever and ever, and cast their crowns before the throne, saying:
"You are worthy, O Lord,
  To receive glory and honor and power;
  For You created all things,
  And by Your will they exist and were created"
    (Rev. 4:10–11).

Responsibility to the Church

Membership

"Again I say to you that if two of you agree on earth concerning anything that they ask, it will be done for them by My Father in heaven" (Matt. 18:19).

Then those who gladly received his word were baptized; and that day about three thousand souls were added *to them.* . . . So continuing daily with one accord in the temple, and breaking bread from house to house, they ate their food with gladness and simplicity of heart, praising God and having favor with all the people. And the Lord added to the church daily those who were being saved (Acts 2:41,46–47)

And the word of God spread, and the number of the disciples multiplied greatly in Jerusalem, and a great many of the priests were obedient to the faith (Acts 6:7).

Therefore, as we have opportunity, let us do good to all, especially to those who are of the household of faith (Gal. 6:10).

Regular Attendance

"I was glad when they said to me,
Let us go into the house of the LORD"
(Ps. 122:1).

And let us consider one another in order to stir up love and good works, not forsaking the assembling of ourselves together, as *is* the manner of some, but exhorting *one another,* and so much the more as you see the Day approaching (Heb. 10:24–25).

Honor all *people.* Love the brotherhood. Fear God. Honor the king (1 Pet. 2:17).

For you, brethren, became imitators of the churches of God which are in Judea in Christ Jesus. For you also suffered the same things from your own

countrymen, just as they *did* from the Jews, . . .
(1 Thess. 2:14).

Financial Support

Honor the LORD with your possessions,
And with the firstfruits of all your increase; . . .
(Prov. 3:9).

"Bring all the tithes into the storehouse,
That there may be food in My house,
And prove Me now in this,"
Says the LORD of hosts,
"If I will not open for you the windows of heaven
And pour out for you *such* blessing
That *there will* not *be room* enough *to receive it"*
    (Mal. 3:10).

On the first *day* of the week let each one of you lay
something aside, storing up as he may prosper, that
there be no collections when I come
(1 Cor. 16:2).

. . . that in a great trial of affliction the abundance
of their joy and their deep poverty abounded in the
riches of their liberality. For I bear witness that
according to *their* ability, yes, and beyond *their*
ability, *they were* freely willing, imploring us with
much urgency that we would receive the gift and
the fellowship of the ministering to the saints. And
this they did, not as we had hoped, but first gave
themselves to the Lord, and *then* to us by the will
of God (2 Cor. 8:2–5).

Corporate Ministry

And when he had found him, he brought him to Antioch. So it was that for a whole year they assembled with the church and taught a great many people. And the disciples were first called Christians in Antioch (Acts 11:26).

. . . strengthening the souls of the disciples, exhorting *them* to continue in the faith, and *saying,* "We must through many tribulations enter the kindom of God" (Acts 14:22).

"Therefore take heed to yourselves and to all the flock, among which the Holy Spirit has made you overseers, to shepherd the church of God which He purchased with His own blood" (Acts 20:28).

If *anyone inquires* about Titus, *he is* my partner and fellow worker concerning you. Or if our brethren *are inquired about, they are* messengers of the churches, the glory of Christ (2 Cor. 8:23).

But you be watchful in all things, endure afflictions, do the work of an evangelist, fulfill your ministry (2 Tim. 4:5).

Let the word of Christ dwell in you richly in all wisdom, teaching and admonishing one another in psalms and hymns and spiritual songs, singing with grace in your hearts to the Lord (Col. 3:16).

═ 20 ═

Community

Every Christian is a citizen of two communities: one spiritual and the other temporal. The believer is both a citizen of heaven and a citizen of earth. Therefore, we have a God-given responsibility to the society in which we live. It is there that we are to show the love of God and the power of Christ to our friends and neighbors. They must see the reality of Christ in our lives in our day-to-day social contact.

Beyond our immediate associates, we have a spiritual and social obligation to the world in general. The Bible exhorts us to care for the needy, visit widows and orphans, minister to prisoners and reach out to the outcasts of society. In so doing we become both the "salt of the earth" and the "light of the world."

You may well be the vital link to someone's salvation. A word fitly spoken, a testimony given or an example displayed, could all be used by God to reach the lost and point them to Christ. God has saved you for the specific purpose of proclaiming the gospel of Christ to

249

others. You have a world of opportunity at your doorstep. Don't miss it!

Neighbors and Friends

Love Them

"'You shall not take vengeance, nor bear any grudge against the children of your people, but you shall love your neighbor as yourself: I *am* the LORD'" (Lev. 19:18).

"Teacher, which *is* the great commandment in the law?" Jesus said to him, "*'You shall love the LORD your God with all your heart, with all your soul, and with all your mind.'* This is *the* first and great commandment. And *the* second *is* like it: *'You shall love your neighbor as yourself.'* On these two commandments hang all the Law and the Prophets" (Matt. 22:36–40).

Jesus answered him, "The first of all the commandments *is: 'Hear, O Israel, the LORD our God, the LORD is one. And you shall love the LORD your God with all your heart, with all your soul, with all your mind, and with all your strength.' This is the first commandment. And the second, like it, is this: 'You shall love your neighbor as yourself.'* There is no other commandment greater than these." So the scribe said to Him, "Well *said,* Teacher. You have spoken the truth, for there is one God, and there is no other but He. And to love Him with all the heart, with all the understanding, with all the soul, and with all the strength, and to love one's neighbor as oneself, is more than all the whole burnt offerings and sacrifices." So when Jesus saw that he answered wisely, He said to him, "You are not far from the kingdom of God." And after that no one dared question Him (Mark 12:29–34).

Love does no harm to a neighbor; therefore love *is* the fulfillment of the law (Rom. 13:10).

Value Them

Do not forsake your own friend or your father's friend,
Nor go to your brother's house in the day of your calamity;
For better *is* a neighbor nearby than a brother far away (Prov. 27:10).

Seldom set foot in your neighbor's house,
Lest he become weary of you and hate you (Prov. 25:17).

He who is devoid of wisdom despises his neighbor.
But a man of understanding holds his peace (Prov. 11:12).

Help Neighbors and Friends

"Everyone helped his neighbor,
And said to his brother,
Be of good courage!" (Isa. 41:6).

" 'Let none of you think evil in your heart against
   your neighbor;
And do not love a false oath.
For all these *are things* that I hate,'
Says the LORD" (Zech. 8:17).

Let each of us please *his* neighbor for *his* good,
leading to edification (Rom. 15:2).

Therefore let us pursue the things *which make* for
peace and the things by which one may edify
another (Rom. 14:19).

. . . just as I also please all *men* in all *things*, not
seeking my own profit, but the *profit* of many, that
they may be saved (1 Cor. 10:33).

Be Honest with Neighbors and Friends
"You shall not bear false witness against your
   neighbor.
You shall not covet your neighbor's house; you shall
   not covet your neighbor's wife, nor his
   manservant, nor his maidservant, nor his ox, nor
   his donkey, nor anything that *is* your neighbor's"
   (Exod. 20:16–17).

He who passes by *and* meddles in a quarrel not his
   own
Is like one who takes a dog by the ears.
Like a madman who throws firebrands, arrows,
   and death,
Is the man *who* deceives his neighbor,
And says, "I was only joking!" (Prov. 26:17–19).

These *are* the things you shall do:
Speak each man the truth to his neighbor;
Give judgment in your gates for truth, justice, and
   peace; . . . (Zech. 8:16).

Care for Neighbors and Friends

But he, wanting to justify himself, said to Jesus,
"And who is my neighbor?" Then Jesus answered
and said: "A certain *man* went down from
Jerusalem to Jericho, and fell among thieves, who
stripped him of his clothing, wounded *him*, and
departed, leaving *him* half dead. Now by chance a
certain priest came down that road. And when he
saw him, he passed by on the other side. Likewise
a Levite, when he arrived at the place, came and
looked, and passed by on the other side. But a
certain Samaritan, as he journeyed, came where he
was. And when he saw him, he had compassion *on
him*, and went to *him* and bandaged his wounds,
pouring on oil and wine; and he set him on his
own animal, brought him to an inn, and took care
of him. On the next day, when he departed, he
took out two denarii, gave *them* to the innkeeper,
and said to him, 'Take care of him; and whatever
more you spend, when I come again, I will repay
you.' So which of these three do you think was
neighbor to him who fell among the thieves?" And
he said, "He who showed mercy on him." Then
Jesus said to him, "Go and do likewise"
(Luke 10:29–37).

People in General

Love Them

"You shall neither mistreat a stranger nor oppress him, for you were strangers in the land of Egypt" (Exod. 22:21).

Do not forget to entertain strangers, for by so *doing* some have unwittingly entertained angels (Heb. 13:2).

"Therefore love the stranger, for you were strangers in the land of Egypt" (Deut. 10:19).

Be Kind to Them

I *was* eyes to the blind,
And I *was* feet to the lame (Job 29:15).

Pure and undefiled religion before God and the Father is this: to visit orphans and widows in their trouble, *and* to keep oneself unspotted from the world (James 1:27).

Remember the prisoners as if chained with them, *and* those who are mistreated, since you yourselves are in the body also (Heb. 13:3).

A man has joy by the answer of his mouth,
And a word *spoken* in due season, how good *it is!*
   (Prov. 15:23).

Pleasant words *are like* a honeycomb,
Sweetness to the soul and health to the bones
   (Prov. 16:24).

He has shown you, O man, what *is* good:
And what does the LORD require of you
But to do justly, to love mercy,
And to walk humbly with your God? (Mic. 6:8).

Treat People Equally

"You shall follow what is altogether just, that you
may live and inherit the land which the LORD your
God is giving you" (Deut. 16:20).

The curse of the LORD *is* on the house of the
 wicked,
But He blesses the habitation of the just (Prov. 3:33).

These *things* also *belong* to the wise:
It is not good to show partiality in judgment
 (Prov. 24:23).

To do righteousness and justice
Is more acceptable to the LORD than sacrifice
 (Prov. 21:3).

The rich and the poor have this in common,
The LORD *is* the maker of them all (Prov. 22:2).

Hate evil, love good;
Establish justice in the gate.
It may be that the LORD God of hosts
Will be gracious to the remnant of Joseph
 (Amos 5:15).

Masters, give your servants what is just and fair,
knowing that you also have a Master in heaven
(Col. 4:1).

Then Peter opened *his* mouth and said: "In truth I perceive that God shows no partiality" (Acts 10:34).

"Yet it shall not be so among you; but whoever desires to become great among you, let him be your servant" (Matt. 20:26).

For there is no distinction between Jew and Greek, for the same Lord over all is rich to all who call upon Him (Rom. 10:12).

Live Your Testimony Before All People
Come *and* hear, all you who fear God,
And I will declare what He has done for my soul
   (Ps. 66:16).

"You are the salt of the earth; but if the salt loses its flavor, how shall it be seasoned? It is then good for nothing but to be thrown out and trampled underfoot by men. You are the light of the world. A city that is set on a hill cannot be hidden. Nor do they light a lamp and put it under a basket, but on a lampstand, and it gives light to all *who are* in the house. Let your light so shine before men, that they may see your good works and glorify your Father in heaven" (Matt. 5:13–16).

"Also I say to you, whoever confesses Me before men, him the Son of Man also will confess before the angels of God" (Luke 12:8).

"But when the Helper comes, whom I shall send to you from the Father, the Spirit of truth who

Community

proceeds from the Father, He will testify of Me.
And you also will bear witness, because you have
been with *Me* from the beginning" (John 15:26–27).

"For we cannot but speak the things which we have
seen and heard" (Acts 4:20).

Now all things *are* of God, who has reconciled us to
Himself through Jesus Christ, and has given us the
ministry of reconciliation, that is, that God was in
Christ reconciling the world to Himself, not
imputing their trespasses to them, and has
committed to us the word of reconciliation.
Therefore we are ambassadors for Christ, as though
God were pleading through us: we implore *you* on
Christ's behalf, be reconciled to God (2 Cor.
5:18–20).

For our gospel did not come to you in word only,
but also in power, and in the Holy Spirit and in
much assurance, as you know what kind of men we
were among you for your sake. . . . so that you
became examples to all in Macedonia and Achaia
who believe (1 Thess. 1:5,7).

Moreover he must have a good testimony among
those who are outside, lest he fall into reproach
and the snare of the devil (1 Tim. 3:7).

For this reason I also suffer these things;
nevertheless I am not ashamed, for I know whom I
have believed and am persuaded that He is able to

keep what I have committed to Him until that Day
(1 Tim. 4:12).

And a servant of the Lord must not quarrel but be
gentle to all, able to teach, patient, in humility
correcting those who are in opposition, if God
perhaps will grant them repentance, so that they
may know the truth, and *that* they may come to
their senses *and escape* the snare of the devil, having
been taken captive by him to *do* his will
(2 Tim. 2:24–26).

. . . in all things showing yourself *to be* a pattern of
good works; in doctrine *showing* integrity,
reverence, incorruptibility, sound speech that
cannot be condemned, that one who is an
opponent may be ashamed, having nothing evil to
say of you (Titus 2:7–8).

Bring People to Christ

"Again I say to you that if two of you agree on
earth concerning anything that they ask, it will be
done for them by My Father in heaven. For where
two or three are gathered together in My name, I
am there in the midst of them" (Matt. 28:19–20).

"Then the master said to the servant, 'Go out into
the highways and hedges, and compel *them* to come
in, that my house may be filled'" (Luke 14:23).

"But you shall receive power when the Holy Spirit
has come upon you; and you shall be witnesses to

Me in Jerusalem, and in all Judea and Samaria, and to the end of the earth" (Acts 1:8).

Then Jesus said to them again, "Peace to you! As the Father has sent Me, I also send you" (John 20:21).

Appendix
A Survey of Bible Families

ADAM AND EVE (Gen. 1–5)

The first family in the Bible resulted from the marriage of Adam and Eve. Their sinful disobedience plunged the entire human race into sin, but they were also the first couple to be redeemed by God's grace. In their personal experiences we see a microcosm of all human families. They experienced both great joy and sorrow in their children. The jealous Cain murdered his brother Abel and eventually fathered a line of rebellious and ungodly people. But the righteous Seth fathered a line of long-living godly people.

NOAH'S FAMILY (Gen. 6–10)

Noah's wife is unnamed in Scripture, but his three sons are clearly identified as the forefathers of the world's great races that developed after the flood. Shem was the forefather of the Semitic peoples, including Israel. Ham was the forefather of both Asians and Africans. Japheth was the forefather of the Europeans. All of them were blessed by Noah's simple obedience to God's command to build the ark.

JOB'S FAMILY (Job 1–42)

Job was one of the greatest men of the ancient East. A semi-nomadic herdsman, Job lost his ten children and his entire wealth in one day of incredible personal disaster. Next, he lost his health. In all his grief he refused to blame God, but announced, "The Lord gave, and the Lord has taken away; blessed be the name of the Lord" (Job 1:21). Though his wife nearly broke under this pressure and his own friends condemned him, Job retained his faith in God and was eventually restored to long life, double prosperity and ten more children. He is undoubtedly the greatest example of patience in the Bible.

ABRAHAM AND SARAH (Gen. 11–25)

Originally known as Abram and Sarai, Abraham ("father of a multitude") and Sarah ("princess") were the parents of the Jewish race through their son Isaac. Abraham is cited in the Bible for his *faith* (see Romans 4:1–5) and Sarah for her *obedience* (see 1 Peter 3:6). Though Abraham also fathered Ishmael by Sarah's handmaid Hagar, God made His covenant with Isaac as the rightful heir to the line of the Messiah.

ISAAC AND REBEKAH (Gen. 21–28)

Abraham's servant found Rebekah among their relatives in Haran and brought her to Canaan to marry Isaac. Though the arrangement was made by the servant, the Scripture clearly indicates that he was led of God in his choice. Their story contains the beautiful footnote: "And she became his wife; and he loved her" (Gen. 24:67).

JACOB'S FAMILY (Gen. 28–49)

Jacob was the youngest of twin brothers. Esau was his life-long rival from whom he wrested both the birthright and the blessing. Fleeing his brother's wrath, Jacob went to Haran where he fell in love with his cousin Rachel for whom he had to wait for seven years only to be tricked into marrying her sister Leah. He then married Rachel one week later, setting the stage for rivalry and jealousy from which his family never fully recovered. Nevertheless, his twelve sons became the forefathers of the twelve tribes of Israel. Despite his early failures, Jacob became a greatly respected father.

JUDAH AND TAMAR (Gen. 38)

Judah was the forefather of the tribe of Judah, the line of David and the line of the Messiah, despite his illegitimate relationship to his widowed daughter-in-law, Tamar. She bore him twin sons Perez and Zerah, but their descendants had to wait for ten generations according to Old Testament Law (see Deuteronomy 23:2) before David came to the throne of Israel (see Ruth 4:18–22). Though they were never legally married, their story is one of God's great grace and forgiveness.

Appendix: Bible Families

JOSEPH'S FAMILY (Gen. 37, 39–50)

Sold into slavery by his jealous brothers, Joseph rose to prominence as the prime minister of Egypt, where he married Asenath, the daughter of an Egyptian priest. God blessed their union with two sons, Manasseh and Ephraim, who became forefathers of two of the tribes of Israel when Joseph received the double portion of the blessing from his father, Jacob. Interestingly, as in his own situation with Esau, Jacob blessed the younger son, Ephraim, over the elder son, Manasseh.

MOSES' FAMILY (Exod. 1–18)

Moses was born of the tribe of Levi while the Israelites were in bondage in Egypt. To spare his life, his mother set him adrift in a basket on the Nile River, where he was found and raised by Pharaoh's daughter with all the privileges of a royal prince. When he later fled Egypt, he met and married Zipporah, the daughter of Reul (Jethro), the priest of Midian. They had two sons, Gershom and Eliezer.

JOSHUA'S FAMILY (Josh. 1–24)

Joshua was originally one of the twelve spies Moses sent into the land of Canaan (cf. Numbers 13:8; 14:6). His skills as a military leader were demonstrated by his victories over the Amalekites (see Exodus 17:13), Midianites (see Numbers 31) and Moabites (see Deuteronomy 3). After Moses' death, Joshua led the children of Israel in the conquest of Canaan, the "Promised Land." Although we know very little about his family, he is well known for his farewell address to the tribes of Israel when he said: "Choose for yourselves this day whom you will serve. . . . But as for me and my house, we will serve the Lord" (Josh. 24:15).

DEBORAH'S FAMILY (Judg. 4–5)

Deborah, the wife of Lapidoth, was one of Israel's first female leaders. The Bible calls her a "prophetess" who "judged" Israel (see Judges 4:4). Therefore, she is generally counted as one of Israel's judges. She rose to prominence during a time when there was a dearth of male leadership in Israel. She virtually had to provoke fellow Israelite Barak into defending Israel from their Canaanite overlord Jabin and his general, Sisera. Together Deborah and Barak won a great victory at the Kishon River when God overpowered the Canaanites with a flash flood.

GIDEON'S FAMILY (Judg. 6–9)

Gideon is best known as the reluctant and fearful leader who defeated the Midianites with a band of only three hundred men. He took a stand for God when he cut down his father's Baal altar and rallied the Israelites against the Midianites. The Bible says: "Gideon had seventy sons who were his own offspring, for he had many wives" (Judges 8:30). After his death, all but one of his sons were killed

by Abimelech, the son of his concubine
(see Judges 9:5).

JEPHTHAH'S FAMILY (Judg. 11)

Jephthah was a son of a harlot in Gilead. He was
later expelled by his step-brothers and cut off from
his father's inheritance. However, when the
Ammonites attacked, the elders of Gilead called
him home and made him captain of their army. As
he rode into battle, Jephthah vowed to God that
whatever came out of his house to meet him would
be sacrificed to God. When he returned victorious
from battle, his daughter and only child ran out to
meet him and the vow was fulfilled when she was
dedicated to a life of perpetual virginity
(see Judges 11:37–39).

SAMSON'S ILL-FATED MARRIAGE
(Judg. 13–16)

Despite being the strongest man who ever lived,
Samson's life was marked by two major tragedies,
one of which was his ill-fated marriage to the
Philistine woman of Timnah (see Judges 14) and the
other, his disastrous relationship with Delilah of
Sorek (see Judges 16). Samson was both a Nazarite
and a judge of Israel, who, in spite of his parents'
objection, was determined to marry the Philistine
woman of Timnah, only to be betrayed by her at
the wedding reception. When he left, angry, she
was given to the best man instead. Samson later
burned their fields in spite and the Philistines in

turn burned the woman and her father
(see Judges 15:6).

BOAZ AND RUTH (Ruth 1–4)

The story of Boaz and Ruth's courtship is one of
the great love stories of the Bible. Ruth was a
Moabite girl who had been widowed by the death
of Mahlon, her Jewish husband. Because of her
devotion to her mother-in-law, Naomi, Ruth
returned with her to her native town of Bethlehem.
There she met and married the mighty and wealthy
Boaz, who became her kinsman to redeem her out
of widowhood. Their firstborn son was Obed, the
grandfather of David. Thus, they helped perpetuate
the line of Christ.

SAMUEL'S FAMILY (1 Sam. 1–12)

The prophet Samuel was born to Elkanah and
Hannah when she promised to give her son to God
if He would bless her with conception (see
1 Samuel 1:11). As a child, Samuel was taken to Eli
the priest to serve the Lord in the Tabernacle of
Israel. Even when Samuel was young, all Israel
"knew that Samuel had been established as a
prophet of the Lord" (1 Sam. 3:20). Despite his
faithfulness to God, the Bible tells us that his sons
"did not walk in his ways" but "took bribes, and
perverted justice" (1 Sam. 8:3). However, in his last
years, Samuel was able to clear his sons by offering
to repay any money taken wrongfully (see 1 Samuel

12:1–4). Here is a beautiful picture of a good family gone wrong and set right again.

SAUL'S FAMILY (1 Sam. 9–13)

Saul was from one of the prominent families of the tribe of Benjamin. Taller than anyone else in Israel, he was the people's choice to be their first king. However, he was an ineffective leader whose bitterness and jealousy toward David destroyed him. He was estranged from his son Jonathan, who remained loyal to David. Saul also constantly interfered with his daughter Michal's marriage to David, finally urging her to leave David for another man. Without David to defend him, Saul eventually died in battle against the Philistines. Several years after his death, two of his sons and five of his grandsons were put to death because of his sins (see 2 Samuel 21:1–9).

DAVID'S FAMILY (1 Samuel 17–31; 1 Kings 2)

While David was Israel's greatest warrior and king, he was somewhat less than an ideal husband and father. His incredible victory over Goliath won him the dubious honor of marriage to Saul's daughter Michal. Though she initially loved him (see 1 Samuel 18:28), she later became estranged from him because of her father's constant interference in their marriage. David later married Abigail, Ahinoam and four other wives. He then fell into adultery with Bathsheba whom he eventually married and by whom he fathered Solomon. His later years were marked by several tragedies, including the death of his infant son by Bathsheba, the murder of his son Amnon by Amnon's step-brother Absalom and Absalom's subsequent rebellion and death. Nevertheless, David lived to be seventy and ruled Israel for forty years.

SOLOMON'S FAMILY (1 Kings 2–11)

Solomon was the legitimate son of David and Bathsheba who came to the throne of Israel during the greatest years of her peace and prosperity. He is best remembered for his wisdom, exemplified in Proverbs, Ecclesiastes and the Song of Solomon, and the fact that he built the Temple in Jerusalem. However, his multiple marriage alliances to foreign wives, including Pharaoh's daughter, spiritually weakened the nation. In all he had seven hundred wives and three hundred concubines who "turned away his heart" from God (see 1 Kings 11:3). After his death, his kingdom was divided when his servant Jeroboam rebelled against his son Rehoboam.

AHAB AND JEZEBEL (1 Kings 16–22; 2 Kings 9)

Ahab ruled the northern kingdom of Israel at Samaria for twenty-two years. He was an ungodly king who married the wicked Jezebel, a Phoenecian princess, who promoted the worship of Baal. They eventually engineered the death of Naboth, a godly landowner, which brought the wrath of God upon them. They were opposed by the fiery prophet Elijah who defeated the prophets of Baal on Mount Carmel and predicted the couple's violent deaths. "The dogs will lick your blood," he told Ahab, and added, "The dogs shall eat Jezebel by the wall of Jezreel" (see 1 Kings 21:19, 23). Both prophecies were literally fulfilled (see 1 Kings 22:38 and 2 Kings 9:36). Eventually Ahab's entire family was slaughtered and his dynasty cut off.

NAAMAN'S FAMILY (2 Kings 5)

Naaman was the captain of the Syrian army, which was an enemy of Israel. He was a man of great power and authority but had contracted leprosy. He and his wife had an Israelite servant girl who had been captured in battle. She told them about the prophet Elisha and his power to heal. In faith, Naaman journeyed to Israel to meet the prophet who told him to dip himself seven times in the Jordan River and he would be healed. When he did as he was told, he was instantly healed and believed "there is no God in all the earth, except in Israel" (2 Kings 5:15).

ISAIAH AND THE PROPHETESS (Isa. 7–8)

Isaiah was the greatest literary prophet of the Old Testament. He lived in Jerusalem and was a personal advisor to the godly King Hezekiah whom he helped withstand an invasion by Sennacherib, King of Assyria (see Isaiah 36–37). The prophet's wife is simply called "the prophetess" in Scripture. She was the mother of his symbolically named children Mahershalalhashbaz ("speed the spoil, hasten the prey") and Shear-jashub ("the remnant shall return").

HOSEA AND GOMER (Hos. 1–14)

Hosea was a prophet to Israel in the last days of the northern kingdom. God led him to marry a woman named Gomer, who became unfaithful and bore two children that were not his. God named them Loruhamah ("no mercy") and Loammi ("not my people"). They became symbolic of God's dealings with Israel whom He was about to cast off. Gomer herself sunk so low that she was sold into sexual slavery, and Hosea had to buy her back for fifteen pieces of silver. Despite her adulteries, Hosea never gave up on her and loved her anyway. His love for his unfaithful wife became a picture of God's love for unfaithful Israel and His willingness to forgive her.

AHASUERUS AND ESTHER (Esther 1–10)

Ahasuerus, known to the Greeks as Xerxes I, ruled the Persian Empire from 485–464 B.C. During his reign he deposed Vashti his queen and conducted a beauty contest to find a new wife. Esther was a Jewish girl whose family had been taken captive by the Babylonians years before. She not only won the contest and became his queen, but she also risked her life to save her people, the

Jews, from the scourge of Haman. Encouraged by her cousin Mordecai, she dared to enter the king's presence without an invitation and wisely won him over to the cause of the Jews. Her story reveals God's providential care for His people while they were in captivity.

ZACHARIAS AND ELIZABETH (Luke 1)

The New Testament opens with the story of the parents of John the Baptist. Zacharias was a priest serving in the temple when an angel appeared to him to announce that he and his wife would have a son despite their advancing years. Elizabeth was the cousin of Mary, the mother of Jesus. When Mary visited Elizabeth, the unborn child John "leaped" within Elizabeth's womb in the presence of the newly conceived Christ (see Luke 1:41). Together they rejoiced at what God had miraculously done for them. In the meantime, Zacharias was struck speechless until John was born. In time their son became the forerunner of Christ.

JOSEPH AND MARY (Matthew 1–2; Luke 1–2)

The finest marriage recorded in Scripture was undoubtedly that of Joseph and Mary, the mother of Jesus. Joseph is described as a "just man" (see Matthew 1:19) and Mary as a "virgin . . . highly favored . . . blessed among women" (Luke 1:27–28). The Holy Spirit came upon her while she was a virgin and caused her to conceive Jesus. Though Joseph legally married her, he had no physical relationship with her until after the birth of Christ (see Matthew 1:25). A carpenter by trade, Joseph served as an ideal legal father for Jesus as he grew up in Nazareth. Later, Joseph and Mary had several other children as well (see John 7:3–5). Eventually one of the brothers, James, became the pastor of the Church at Jerusalem and another authored the epistle of Jude.

PETER'S FAMILY (Luke 4:31–39)

We do not know a great deal about Peter's family except that they lived in a house in Capernaum. It was there that Jesus healed Peter's "wife's mother," an event recorded in three places (see Matthew 8:14–15; Mark 1:29–31; Luke 4:38–39). That Peter was married and had a mother-in-law is clearly stated. He earned his living as a fisherman, but eventually forsook all and followed Jesus. It was from his boat that Jesus preached and where the miraculous catch of fish occurred. Eventually Peter both confessed the Lord and denied him, but finally became the apostles' leading spokesman. On the day of Pentecost, three thousand people were converted under his preaching (see Acts 2:41).

LAZARUS' FAMILY (Luke 10:38–42; John 11:1–5)

Lazarus was the brother of Mary and Martha of Bethany. Jesus visited often in their home and loved them all. The two women were a contrast: Martha loved serving the Lord and Mary loved listening to Him (see Luke 10:38–42). When their brother became seriously ill, they sent for Jesus, who delayed His coming until after Lazarus had been dead four days. When he arrived, Jesus announced to Martha, "I am the resurrection and the life" (John 11:25) and asked to be taken to the tomb. He demanded that the stone be removed and shouted with a loud voice, "Lazarus, come forth," and raised Lazarus from the dead. This family's kindness to Jesus was repaid in a manner beyond their wildest hopes.

ANANIAS AND SAPPHIRA (Acts 5)

One of the most tragic stories in the New Testament is that of Ananias and Sapphira who lied to the apostles about their donation to the Church. Claiming they had sold all their possessions, they "kept back part of the proceeds" for themselves (Acts 5:2). When the apostle Peter confronted them about lying to the Holy Spirit, they both fell dead at his feet. Their conspiracy to do wrong cost them their lives.

PHILIP'S FAMILY (Acts 6:1–9:40; 21:1–15)

Philip was an outstanding evangelist who was also one of the original seven deacons selected by the apostles (see Acts 6:5). He conducted a very successful preaching mission in Samaria (see Acts 8:5–8). Then God sent him into the desert strip at Gaza to witness to the Ethiopian eunuch (see Acts 8:26–39). Finally, he preached his way up the Mediterranean coast until he settled at Caesarea

(Acts 8:40). Years later, the apostle Paul visited his home where his four virgin daughters prophesied (Acts 21:8–9). While Paul remained there, Agabus came from nearby Joppa to warn him not to go to Jerusalem. Philip is an example of a family man who was busy sharing the gospel with others throughout his lifetime.

CORNELIUS' FAMILY (Acts 10)

Cornelius was a Roman centurion stationed at Caesarea, the provincial capital. He is described as a family man and a "devout man and one who feared God with all his household" (Acts 10:2). Having seen a vision, he sent for Peter at nearby Joppa. Peter went to Caesarea, announcing: "God shows no partiality" and preached to the Gentiles assembled there. As he preached, the Holy Spirit came upon them and they were baptized. Thus, the mission of Gentile evangelism began with this one family.

LYDIA'S FAMILY (Acts 16:14–15)

When the apostle Paul arrived in the Greek city of Philippi, he attended a Sabbath day riverside prayer meeting where Lydia, "a seller of purple," heard him and was converted. She was a native of Thyatira in Asia Minor (see Revelation 2:18). The Bible says, "she and her household were baptized" and that she opened her home in hospitality to the apostles.

Appendix: Bible Families

AQUILA AND PRISCILLA (Acts 18:1–26)

When Paul arrived in Corinth, he met two fellow tentmakers named Aquila and Priscilla. They were Jews who had been expelled from Rome by Emperor Claudius (see Acts 18:2). They became converts and followed Paul to Ephesus. There they later instructed Apollos in "the way of God more accurately" (Acts 18:26). In Paul's epistle to the Corinthians, he brings a salutation from Aquila and Priscilla and the "church that is in their house" (1 Cor. 16:19). In his epistle to the Romans, Paul says, "Greet Priscilla and Aquila, my fellow workers in Christ Jesus" (Rom. 16:3). It is obvious that this couple got around a lot and that they hosted a church assembly in their own home.

TIMOTHY'S FAMILY (Acts 16:1–3; 2 Timothy 1:5)

Timothy was Paul's spiritual son in the faith. His father was Greek and his mother Jewish. They lived in Lystra in Asia Minor and were converted during Paul's second missionary journey (see Acts 16:1–3). In commenting on his family background, Paul said, "I call to remembrance the genuine faith that is in you, which first dwelt in your grandmother Lois and your mother Eunice" (2 Timothy 1:5). Timothy accompanied Paul on several of his evangelistic endeavors and later pastored the Church at Ephesus. He was the recipient of a great spiritual family heritage.

TITUS' FAMILY (Titus 1–3)

Paul also referred to Titus as "my true son in our common faith" (Titus 1:4). He was the pastor of the Church on the island of Crete. Speaking directly to him, Paul said that a bishop must be "a man blameless, the husband of one wife, having faithful children" (Titus 1:6). In describing the ideal family, Paul wrote to Titus that mature men should be "sober, reverent, temperate, sound in faith, in love, in patience" (Titus 2:2). He added that mature women should be "reverent in behavior, not slanderers, not given to much wine . . . discreet, chaste, homemakers, good, obedient to their husbands" (Titus 2:3–5). As such, Paul was describing the ideal Christian family, which is the foundation for the ideal pastor's family.

Notes

Notes

Notes

Notes

Notes

Notes